Introduction

There are two compelling moral reasons for U.S. concern about the conditions under which political prisoners are held in south Viet Nam. First, Americans bear a direct and major responsibility for the arrest, confinement and treatment of prisoners in south Viet Nam. Tens of thousands of civilians were taken prisoner by U.S. military personnel and turned over to the south Vietnamese police or military. Many of these people are still in jail, and the United States government has acknowledged 'residual responsibility' for them. [1]

In addition, United States officials have known about the brutality in Vietnamese prisons for many years. In a report dated October 1, 1963, and signed by Frank E. Walton, Chief of the Public Safety Division in Saigon, confinement in the discipline cells of Con Son prison was described this way:

> In Con Son II, some of the hardcore communists keep preaching the 'party' line, so these 'Reds' are sent to the Tiger Cages in Con Son I where they are isolated from all others for months at a time. This confinement may also include rice without salt and water--the United States prisons' equivalent of bread and water. It may include immobilization--the prisoner is bolted to the floor, handcuffed to a bar or rod, or legirons with the chain through an eyebolt, or around a bar or rod.

For these reasons, Americans should be alarmed at the increasingly frequent reports that political prisoners are being tortured and killed in the jails of the Saigon government. They are detained by a police force which we finance, confined in prisons which we built and interrogated by individuals we trained and still advise. These actions must cease. These people, whose only crime is to oppose the Thieu government, must be released. The United States must end its support of a police apparatus which terrorizes a nation.

Secondly, Americans should be concerned about the treatment and release of political prisoners if they want to end the war and stop the suffering of all the Vietnamese people--rather than just get the United States out of combat. The Thieu regime holds thousands of prisoners from high school students to pacifist Buddhists, from elected National Assembly members to National Liberation Front cadre. If legal political activity continues to be defined solely by the Thieu regime, then the war is bound to go on.

Many of those currently imprisoned represent the middle of the political spectrum. Their outlook lies between that of the Saigon government and the views of the National Liberation Front. After more than a decade of intense and fratricidal war, these people are vital to the success of attempts of accommodation and reconciliation.

We estimate that the number of political prisoners held by the Saigon government exceeds 200,000. That figure is based on information provided by south Vietnamese sources [2] and on the statements of respected outside observers. [3] Whatever the exact number, all political prisoners should be released and guaranteed full political participation in the future of their country. At present the most significant memorial to America's intervention in south Viet Nam is the thousands of political prisoners held in the name of freedom.

[1] *Christian Science Monitor,* July 30, 1971.

[2a] "arrests are continuing at the rate of 14,000 per month..." *Time*, July 10, 1972.

[2b] "On November 9, 1972 Hoang Duc Nha, President Thieu's closest advisor reportedly told a group of Vietnamese publishers that 40,000 communist agents had been arrested throughout the country in the past few weeks." *Washington Post*, November 10, 1972.

[3a] " A reasonable figure is probably at least two hundred thousand civilians in custody of one kind or another in the area of conflict." News Release, Amnesty International, November 2, 1972.

[3b] " The prisoners now thought to be in custody in south Viet Nam allegedly total more than 240,000 and include students, adults and a number of clergy." News Release, *Anglican News Service* (Canadian), December 14, 1972.

[3c] " He (Ngo Cong Duc, former legislator and former President of the Saigon publishers Association) put the total number of political prisoners in south Viet Nam at 200,000." *New York Times*, September 7, 1972.

The Laws

RESTRICTIONS ON INDIVIDUALS

The incarceration of a large number of prisoners has always been characteristic of the Saigon government. Over fifty thousand political prisoners were held by the Diem regime when it was overthrown by the United States government and the Saigon military for "being out of touch with the people" [1] of south Viet Nam. But successive governments have arrested more and more citizens on the basis of their political beliefs. As the political struggle within south Viet Nam has intensified, and the desire for peace has increased among the population, the number of political prisoners has grown dramatically.

The south Vietnamese government and its American advisors have attempted to defend the legality of all of these arrests. But the list of punishable violations, the regulations governing evidence, and the methods of sentencing reveal a system designed to permit the imprisonment of anyone the government wants to get rid of.

DECREE-LAWS

Decree-Laws are issued by the executive branch of the government. They are supposed to be approved by consent of the legislature, but irregularities often attend this procedure. For example, the latest set of Decree-Laws granted what one newspaper called "unlimited power" [2] in the areas of defense, security, economics and finance. They were passed in a special session of the Senate which was held after curfew, when all of the opponents of the bill were absent.

As the following examples indicate, Decree-Laws are characterized by severe penalties and prohibit almost all types of political activities. (Summary titles added for clarification)

NEUTRALISM EQUALS PRO-COMMUNIST NEUTRALISM

Number 93/SL/CT

Article 1: By this Decree are outlawed private persons, parties, leagues, associations that commit acts of any form which are, directly or indirectly, aimed at practicing Communism or Pro-Communist Neutralism.

Article 2: Shall be considered as Pro-Communist Neutralist a person who commits acts of propaganda for and incitement of Neutralism; these acts are assimilate to acts of jeopardizing public security. (Note of the translator: The act of jeopardizing public security is punished by Article 91 para 3 of the South Viet Nam Revised Code of Criminal Laws with a maximum penalty of 5 years imprisonment).

LIFE IMPRISONMENT AT HARD LABOR FOR DEMONSTRATIONS

Number 004/65

Article 16: Is sentenced to solitary confinement with hard labor for life any person who excites the mob by organizing meetings or demonstrations with the purpose to disturb the security of the state.

YEARS OF HARD LABOR FOR UNDERMINING ANTI-COMMUNIST SPIRIT

Number 004/65

Article 17: Is sentenced to hard labor for a term of years any person...who commits any act in order to undermine the anti-communist spirit of the country, or to cause harmful effect to the struggle of the people and the Armed Forces.

[1-1] President John F. Kennedy, interview with Walter Cronkite, *CBS*, September 2, 1963

[1-2] *Washington Star,* June 29, 1972

DETAINED IF <u>CONSIDERED</u> DANGEROUS TO NATIONAL SECURITY

Number 018/64

<u>Article 1</u>: During the State of Emergency and from the date of promulgation, this Decree-Law onwards, the following measures will be applied:

--Order the detention of or assign residence to those elements who are considered as dangerous to the national security.

DEATH PENALTY FOR RESISTING PUBLIC FORCE PERSONNEL

Number 004/66

<u>Article 22</u>: Those persons who gather in assemblage of two or more and attack, resist or <u>obstruct</u> the public force personnel in their duties shall be punished with death.

The killing of offenders in self defense shall be excused.

Though these laws allow the south Vietnamese government to arrest almost anyone who expresses active or verbal opposition to official policies, the Saigon regime issued another Decree-Law which grants it even more power. This article is known in Viet Nam as the <u>antri law</u>. Because it requires no trial and no appeal is permitted, it is the most frequently invoked Decree-Law.

PEOPLE CAN BE HELD TWO YEARS WITHOUT TRIAL...WHICH IS RENEWABLE

Number 004/66

<u>Article 19</u>: Those persons considered dangerous to the national defense and public security may be interned in a prison or designated area, or banished from designated areas for a maximum period of two years, which is renewable.

PRESS CENSORSHIP

Freedom of the press has fared no better than individual freedom in south Viet Nam. Severe censorship and seizure of Saigon's newspapers has prevailed for years. But a new Decree-Law issued on June 15, 1972, threatens to close down all press and periodicals except those that completely support the government. Article 10 of this law reads: "...those who popularize, possess or circulate those publications, leaflets, information and news, or photographs deemed harmful to national security, will be severly punished." The result of this law has been a rash of fines and jail terms for Saigon newsmen. For example on July 7, 1972:

The south Vietnamese government announced that 42 sentences had been meted out since June 22 against Vietnamese newspapermen, including heavy fines and prison terms up to one month.

Of 57 cases brought against newspapermen by the government, there were convictions in all but 15. In no case did the government disclose what the newsmen's special offenses had been.[3]

On September 24, 1972, additional fines and closing of opposition newspapers were reported.

One of Saigon's two remaining opposition newspapers has been heavily fined and one of its executives sentenced to a year's imprisonment for having published a report on a Cornell University study on American bombing in Indochina.

In a three-hour trial yesterday, a military tribunal found the Saigon daily, <u>Dien Tin</u>, guilty of "damaging national security" by having published the article last Aug. 16.

[1-3] *New York Times*, July 7, 1972

The newspaper was ordered to forfeit one-million piasters, about $2,320, from a 20-million piaster bond it was recently forced to post with the government.[4]

A subsequent Decree-Law was issued requiring all publications to post nearly $50,000 with the Saigon government to cover future fines for printing unauthorized material. Since most publications couldn't possibly meet such a requirement, the opposition press was eliminated without the formality of a trial. On September 16, 1972, the new law went into effect.

> South Viet Nam's opposition press was virtually silenced today with the permanent closing of 14 daily newspapers and 15 other periodicals that failed to pay large bonds demanded by the government of President Nguyen Van Thieu.
>
> In a decree on Aug. 4, President Thieu ordered all south Vietnamese newspapers and many of the nation's other periodicals to post bonds equivalent to $47,000 each. The deadline passed today. In a speech, Mr. Thieu had made it plain that his intention was to drive many of the publications out of business and it was clear today that the plan had succeeded.
>
> The amount of money involved proved too great for many of the publications, which operated on very small budgets. The government demanded the bonds as guarantees against possible fines to be levied against publications that violated the press code.
>
> Under the new code, virtually any criticism of the government or the armed forces is punishable by confiscation of issues, fines and prison terms for publishers, editors, and reporters, and possible permanent closing.[5]

On that one day, a total of 92 south Vietnamese publications (counting weekly and monthly magazines) were shut down.[6]

President Thieu charged on August 11, 1972, that the communists were "taking advantage of the disorderly and broad-based freedom and democracy in the south." The Decree-Laws of June, 1972 and the rigor with which they have been enforced show that President Thieu intends to tighten his dictorial controls.

As Information Minister Truong Buu Diem said, when asked if papers would be permitted to criticize the government, "Sure, if they do it right."[7]

[1-4] *New York Times*, September 24, 1972

[1-5] *New York Times*, September 16, 1972

[1-6] *Los Angeles Times*, September 16, 1972

[1-7] *Newsday*, August 7, 1972

The Police

A pervasive and repressive police network now operates at every level of south Vietnamese society. More than a dozen military and civilian agencies are legally authorized to make arrests. [1] But, as one Vietnamese Senator observed, "anyone in Viet Nam with a gun can pick people up." [2] Though the national police network includes both military and civilian branches, there is little difference in objectives and procedures between the two. In 1971 the police bureaucracy was removed from the regular civil service and made into a separate military command. Its head, an army officer, is now responsible to President Thieu, rather than a civilian ministry. [3] This combination of civilian police and military functions reflects the views of Robert Thompson, President Nixon's top advisor on counter-insurgency. [4] It also serves the objectives of U.S. Agency for International Development which funds most of Saigon's police activities. [5]

National Police

The largest south Vietnamese police agency is the National Police force. It has increased from 16,000 men in 1963 to over 120,000 by the end of 1972, and further increases are planned. Representatives of the National Police are now stationed in every district in south Viet Nam.

The growth and sophistication of the National Police has been accomplished by a decade of American planning, advising and funding. U.S. economic assistance to the National Police has grown steadily over the last four years. With this funding the police have developed techniques of control which have now reached totalitarian dimensions. Responsibilities of the National Police force now range from identifying and keeping dossiers on every citizen over 15 to the interogation of most prisoners.

The Special Police

The Special Police, a branch of the National Police, are responsible for eliminating NLF cadre and repressing all movements for peace and neutrality. They are especially feared and hated because of their practice of infiltrating opposition political groups and torturing arrested suspects. The mass arrests of 1972 were carried out by the Special Police.

The Active-Service Police

This service forms part of the National Police Force for administrative purposes, but actually receives orders directly from the President's office, from the American Central Intelligence Agency, from the Chiefs of Staff of the south Vietnamese Army, and from the American Special Forces.

More than 20 provincial offices come under this branch of the police. In Saigon alone there are eight offices, employing 80 to 120 people each, not counting the personnel of the 200 to 300 bureaus and all the informers.

2-1 *Washington Post,* September 15, 1968

2-2 *Ibid.*

2-3 *New York Times*, June 23, 1972

2-4 *New Statesman,* October 8, 1972

2-5 " As one aspect of Vietnamization, the Vietnamese National Police are called upon to carry a progressively breater burden. They must share with the Vietnamese armed forces the burden of countering insurgency and provide for daily peace and order -- not only in the cities but in the countryside. Preface to *Fiscal Year 1972 AID Presentation*

The Order Police

The Order Police, another branch of the National Police, are charged with assisting in the quelling of "demonstrations, disorders, and riots..."[6]   Such action was specifically praised in the United States AID report for 1970.

> During 1970 the police continued to improve their capability in traditional police functions. Their timely and positive action effectively contained civil disturbances involving war veterans, students and religious groups, thereby preventing the spread of violence. [7]

No mention was made of the fact that the veterans were disabled while fighting for the Saigon regime and were asking for higher benefits and better medical care. Neither was it mentioned that the students were asking for peace. Such sentiments are not legal in south Viet Nam.

The National Police Field Forces

The National Police Field Force (NPFF) is "a paramilitary police unit engaged primarily in combating the Vietcong Infrastructure (VCI) in rural areas in south Vietnam."[8]   The U.S. Army calls it a "relatively new and major police adjustment in counterinsurgency work."[9]   Their equipment, including tanks and artillery, is identical to that used by the south Vietnamese military forces. Most of their material support comes from the U.S. Department of Defense. The NPFF now numbers more than 25,000 .

Official Saigon Police

The employees of this headquarters can be divided into two categories: uniformed police and plainclothesmen who are granted the right to make arrests. This right becomes an illegal source of income since the innocent but well-off (merchants, restaurant proprietors) are arrested and forced to contribute large sums in order to ensure their release.

The Bureau of Military Security

The Bureau of Military Security is implanted in every unit of the Army and its sphere of action extends to areas surrounding military installations. These units cooperate with the Provost Marshall's Office which on several occasions has directly intervened in the civilian domain, in particular with regard to the arrest of newspapermen and students. The Bureau of Military Security has the right to take action against pacifist intellectuals considered anti-militarist on the basis of their writings or public statements.

The Secret Service

The Secret Service, which works under the direct orders of President Thieu, carries out arrests and executions in all sectors of society. Secret Service agents make use of hired assassins recruited from the Saigon underworld and paid "by the job." Public opinion in Saigon holds the Secret Service responsible for assaults on well-known opponents of the regime.

2-6 *Fiscal Year 1971 AID Program and Project Presentation to Congress* (quoted in NARMIC report *Police on the Homefront*, p. 107.)

2-7 *Fiscal Year 1970 AID Report to the Ambassador*, p. 35

2-8 *Twenty-Second Report,* by the Committee on Government Operations, October 17, 1972, p. 19

2-9 *Area Handbook for South Vietnam*, Department of Army Pamphlet 550-55, p. 414

The Central Intelligence Service

Is headed by American experts and operates entirely on a clandestine basis. At present it is run as a joint American-Vietnamese operation.

The American CIA controls the Central Intelligence Service and also coordinates the operations of the Active Service Police, the Bureau of Military Security and the intelligence bureau at Army headquarters. The Central Intelligence Service is thought to be the center for secret and double agents.

The Resources Control Program

All of these branches of the National Police benefit from the Comprehensive Resources Control Program which has been developed with the aid of American technology. It is designed to "regulate the movement of people and goods" and "restrict the flow of information and supplies." [10]   The Resources Control Program uses the latest technological equipment and techniques for control of the population.

The National Identification Registration Program (NIRP) is under the Resources Control Program and aims to identify and register everyone over 15 years of age.

The project has succeeded in filing almost every Vietnamese into an advanced data bank which was overseen and directed by elements and officers on loan from the FBI. Included in every individual's dossier is a photograph, fingerprints from both hands, a description of the person and "biographic data," including political opinions, personal feelings about the GVN cadres, wealth, family status and any heresay or reputation offered by friends, relatives or informers.[11]

Family Census Program

A similar program is the Family Census, which registers all pertinent data on members of a particular family. A group photo of the entire family is also included. U.S. document prepared for use by American advisors emphasizes that it is vitally important for the National Police to obtain information concerning families since "This can be useful in exploiting family sentiment to obtain his arrest..." [13]

The millions of dollars which have gone to develop Viet Nam's police system have been portrayed to Congress and the American public as a generous contribution to the welfare and protection of the citizens of south Viet Nam. But the actions of the Saigon police forces are as brutal and resented as those of any occupation army. U.S. support for the police forces of the Thieu government has not brought security and stability, but rather, anger, suspicion and fear.

[2-10]Richard Pollack, "Public Safety in Viet Nam: The New Mercenary Force," July 4, 1972, p.4

[2-11]"An Analysis of Provincial Security Committee, (SOP-3), *Congressional Record,* April 21, 1971, p. E3331

The Process of Justice

ARREST

Being arrested in south Viet Nam is more often a matter of chance than of design. The police force has acquired a certain efficiency in repressing political opposition--using massive and indiscriminate arrests rather than precise identification and seizure of suspects.

> It is also impossible to tell how many of those arrested really have communist connections and how many are simply opposed to the government of President Thieu, because the police seem to make little distinction. There is a third category of prisoners as well--people who were apparently seized at random and who committed no crime. They just happened to have been in the wrong place.[1]

As previously stated, over a dozen agencies have the power to arrest people. These agencies include the National Police Force and its branches; the Special Police and the Order Police; the Military Police and its intelligence branch; Local Police; Revolutionary Development Cadre; military officers in charge of military operations; and other secret agencies. Neither a warrant nor firm grounds for suspicion need accompany an arrest.[2]   Only such a vast police network could seize over 40,000 people in a two-week period, as Hoang Duc Nha, President Thieu's closest personal advisor proudly proclaimed on November 9, 1972.[3] Recent reports from south Viet Nam indicate that the Decree-Laws governing national security are now being used to arrest those even remotely suspected of harboring anti-government sentiments. News accounts speak repeatedly of the current series of arrests as being intended to wipe out all political opposition.

In June of 1972 several thousand persons were arrested and shipped to Con Son Island. "In many cases the prisoners were merely relatives of political suspects, many of them women and children."[4]   George Hunter of the San Francisco Examiner reports that:

> Special Branch Police swooped down on houses all over south Viet Nam and arrested anyone under the remotest suspicion of being 'left-wing'...
>
> The government has a blacklist of suspects, but I understand that wives, fathers and mothers--anyone with the slimmest association with those on it are being caught in the net.[5]

A specific example of this wholesale roundup was given in the New York Post.

> On May 25, Trung, a young south Vietnamese writer-translator, who is a polio victim, rode to his parents' house on the back of a friend's scooter. As he swung himself into the house on his crutches, plainclothes police made an arrest. They had been waiting for him in the house for two days, holding his parents, younger brother and a few family visitors.
>
> Before the police took Trung away, one of them mentioned that he was being arrested "because of his writings." Trung protested that they did not have a warrant, but they said that they did not need one since martial law had been declared.

[3-1] *New York Times,* August 13, 1972

[3-2] A summary of the Vietnamese legal system issued to American military legal officers in 1967 justified this procedure in the following fashion: "Since security suspects are particularly likely to learn of an impending arrest and flee, they are commonly arrested without a warrant, although one may be obtained later." *Handbook on National Security: Laws and Procedures*, Saigon, December 1967.

[3-3] *Washington Post,* November 10, 1972

[3-4] *Boston Globe,* June 24, 1972

[3-5] *San Francisco Chronicle,* June 4, 1972

The bulk of Trung's work in the last year was translating material relating to the war from English or French into Vietnamese. Most recently, he was working on The Indochina Story, published by an American group, The Committee of Concerned Asian Scholars. The translation appeared serialized in a Saigon daily paper, and was routinely passed by government censors. [6]

Even Tran Van Tuyen, a prominent Saigon lawyer and a member of the staunchly anti-communist Viet Nam Nationalist Party said, "The administration has taken advantage of the situation to neutralize the opposition. Many of those arrested are not big-name personalities. They are not communists. But they are anti-government." [7] His statement is confirmed by the fact that "most student leaders at the Universities of Hue and Saigon have been arrested." [8]

Others have been interned simply because they lacked proper papers. "Many refugees from fighting zones who have lost their identification papers have been detained on suspicion of being communist infiltrators." [9]

Thus, the mammoth scale of arrests which the south Vietnamese population has endured for years is now being intensified, especially in towns and at universities. Despite increased size and the acquisition of sophisticated equipment, the south Vietnamese police remain as indiscriminately repressive as ever.

DETENTION AND INTERROGATION

Once arrested, a prisoner faces a multitude of dangers. The least serious fate he or she can suffer is having a personal file misplaced. The penalty for this accident can, nevertheless, be quite severe.

> South Viet Nam's antiquated and enormously inefficient judicial system is such that a person can spend years in jail without coming to trial. His dossier perhaps lost in the dusty mountains of archives that characterize national bureaucracy. [10]

Usually, however, the police assume some reason for arrest and treat the subject accordingly. A person may be interned for up to 46 days in order for the government to determine what charges should be placed against him. Though most suspects are detained in Provincial Detention Centers, there is a good chance that at some point in the pre-trial period they will be taken to the Provincial Interrogation Center (PIC), which adjoins the detention center. Since signed confessions are the main evidence used to convict people, it is the Interrogation Center that the suspect may encounter the first officially conducted torture. (Prisoners taken by military units may have been tortured in the field to obtain information of immediate military value.) The prevalence of torture and physical abuse in the interrogation process is substantiated by numerous personal accounts and frequent Congressional inquiries. [11]

A letter smuggled out of Chi Hoa Prison dated October 11, 1972, describes the torture utilized during the interrogation of Saigon student leader Le Cong Giau.

> Le Cong Giau is a science student and former vice secretary general of the executive committee of the Union of Saigon Students (1965-66). Giau was arrested on August 5, 1972, by the Saigon municipal police when leaving a class to return home. The same night, August 5, Giau was taken handcuffed and blind-folded to the office of the

---

[3-6]*New York Post*, June 28, 1972

[3-7]*Christian Science Monitor*, June 23, 1972

[3-8]*Time*, July 10, 1972

[3-9]*New York Times*, June 23, 1972

[3-10]*Ibid.*

[3-11]*The Handbook on National Security: Laws and Procedures* mentions the admissability of confessions and acknowledges that force might have been used to extract them: " Confessions are accepted in evidence, signed by the accused. He may, however, attempt later to show coercion and thus overcome its effect. It is said that a substantial number of convicitions of VC are obtained through confessions."

director of the interrogation center (Mr. Duong Van Chau); also present were lieutenant colonel Nghia, assistant director in charge of the special police, and captain Mai, head of the interrogation, as well as ten interrogation officers. He was immediately subjected to torture and interrogation and forced to admit to having participated in NLF organizations. Giau protested vigorously against the accusations. Nevertheless, he has continually suffered all manner of tortures: persistent beating with a club on the head, chest, shoulders, hands, thighs, knees, legs, and feet. Burning cigarettes were placed on his nipples, navel, and penis; pins were driven into the ends of his fingers. His fingernails and toenails were torn out (this torture was carried out by second lieutenant Duong).

A large quantity of soapy water was forced through his nostrils and mouth until he fainted; then he was kicked in the stomach to force water out (this torture was carried out, once again, by second lieutenant Duong). His hands were tied behind his back, and he was suspended by his feet and beaten savagely with clubs (this torture was carried out by Cu Lu Nhi, a torturer well known in the prison since 1970). Chopsticks were forced up his rectum (torture carried out by Ngoc). The torture was applied from 10 p.m. to 4 a.m. After each session Giau was carried on a board to cell number 2. This particular treatment was imposed every day from the first week of his detention. He is now so weak that he cannot move any of his limbs, and he can only eat by being fed spoonsful of soup by another prisoner. With only a few days break, this interrogation and torture has been systematically carried out for two months. During the week of August 19 to 26, Giau was taken away and hidden in a closed truck so that he would not be seen by an International Red Cross inspection team.

On September 30, one of Giau's fellow prisoners happened to overhear the torturers talking among themselves: "We have never seen anybody as hard to break as this kid (speaking about Giau). We nevertheless use every possible and imaginable technique, but to no avail. He will not talk. There is nothing more we can do but liquidate him.' Giau is now unable to speak. He vomits blood continually; his clothing is so saturated with blood that the cell is filled with an intolerable stench which suffocates even the guards. He is now in a cell covered only by a straw mat. He is lying there like a corpse. On October 1, he was taken to a hospital reserved for combat police to undergo treatment for five days. But, in view of his condition, the chief physician suggested sending him to the civilian hospital, Hong Bang. The director of the interrogation center, Mr. Duong Van Chau, refused to allow this in order to keep the affair secret. Giau was then sent back to the municipal police department to undergo further interrogation. Even in this condition, he has been placed in solitary confinement without being allowed to receive the supplies and medicines brought by his family and friends.

We wish to alert public opinion to the imminent death of Le Cong Giau.

Prisoners of Chi Hoa, October 11, 1972.

Such treatment is not unusual. The following statement was made by a woman who had been imprisoned in the Police Detention Center in Saigon.

"When you were being interrogated, you could hear the screams of people being tortured. Sometimes they showed the torture going on, to try to frighten you into saying what they wanted you to say.

"Two women in my cell were pregnant. One was beaten badly another woman was beaten mostly on the knees, which became infected.

"One high school student tried to kill herself by cutting both wrists on the metal water taps in the washroom, but she failed. They had tortured her by putting some kind of thick rubber band around her head to squeeze it. It made her eyes swell out and gave her unbearable headaches.

"One girl was so badly tortured that the police left her in a corridor outside the interrogation room for a day--so that other prisoners would not see her condition."[12]

3-12 *New York Times*, August 13, 1972

Severity of treatment during interrogation is not simply a recent development brought on by the pressure of current military situation. In a letter dated August, 1969, Grace Kleinbach, M.D. cited the case of a victim of interrogation torture whom she happened to meet in a rural clinic.

> Yesterday on my way home from one of my rural clinics, I stopped at another clinic to see if I could get some cholera vaccine for an impending epidemic in many of the livestock in a nearby area. My presence in this second clinic was totally unexpected, and I met a sight there I will never forget. There on the bench sat a woman in her late thirties, with a red, swollen face. With her was a policeman, who told me she was a Viet Cong suspect and had been under "interrogation" for the past three days in a prison just outside of Saigon. She was now being transferred to another prison where questioning would continue.

> I took her into a private examining room and found her to have multiple cuts and bruises on the head, face, body, and in the mouth. She had multiple fractures of the small bones of the hand, a result of having to put her hands out, palms down, and have them beaten with a heavy stick. There were several marks on her back which she stated were a result of electric shocks. I had previously asked the guard to leave to ensure accuracy of her answers and I now sent my interpreter out on a short errand, leaving me alone with the woman. I took this opportunity to talk to her in more detail. When I asked her if most of the prisoners were treated this way, she nodded tearfully. She said she was going down a street in Saigon, and she was stopped and questioned. The officer took her into custody, even though her papers were complete. She was very worried about her husband and children as she had not been able to notify them of her whereabouts even though they live within a few miles of the prison.

> Previously, I had talked with more Vietnamese friends whose identity must remain anonymous but whose character cannot be questioned. One stated that interrogation officers who can elicit the most "information" receive many metals and promotions, and that the easiest way of getting information is to be skilled in the art of torture.

American advisors to South Vietnamese Provincial Interrogation Centers have long known of their effectiveness in gaining evidence. Congressman Paul McCloskey was made unhappily aware of this effectiveness in a conversation with a United States pacification officer.

> When I asked an American pacification officer if the 46 day period of interrogation was not reasonable, he replied, "We've never had to interrogate anyone for 46 days—they've all broken and confessed in 30 days. [13]

The whole pre-trial process is most briefly summed up in a saying popular among the police, "Khong, danh cho co"—"If they are innocent, beat them until they become guilty." [14]

JUDGEMENT AND SENTENCING

The rules and procedures surrounding arrest, detention and sentencing give the government of south Viet Nam an overwhelming advantage over a suspect charged with a political infraction. But the south Vietnamese judicial process makes conviction almost a certainty. Depending on the results of interrogation and the content of military intelligence reports, the detainee may be brought before a military court or he may be referred to the Provincial Security Committee.

If there is sufficient evidence to warrant a trial, then either the regular Military Courts or the Military Field Courts will hear the case. Though both of these courts should technically convene for only military cases, Decree-Laws have directed that all political offenses by tried before military courts. Both military courts consist of 5 military officers. The common standards of justice—admission of evidence, cross-examination and right of counsel—do not exist. The penalties for most offenses coming before the military courts are prescribed by law. Years at hard labor, life imprisonment and death are the usual sentences. The courts determine guilt or innocence, and their decision cannot be appealed. As a humanitarian gesture, death penalties may be appealed to the mercy of President Thieu.

3-13_Congressional Record,_ July 1, 1971, p. E6932

3-14_New York Times,_ August 13, 1972

The government usually stands a good chance of gaining a conviction in the military courts because of the absense of fundamental legal rights. But even if sufficient evidence to merit a trial is lacking, another procedure allows the Saigon government to imprison its opponents. Article 19 of Decree Law 004/66 (the "an tri" law) provides that a person "considered dangerous to the national defense and public security" may be interned for a period of up to two years. This sentence is renewable. A document entitled "An Analysis of PSC's" for use by United States Military advisors in south Viet Nam summarizes the function of the "an tri" law and the Provisional Security Committees.

> Province Security Committee (PSC) were created in 1957 to provide the GVN with an administrative method of settling the status of political detainees considered threats to the national security. Their purpose is political; their method is administrative detention of those persons reasonably believed to endanger the national security, but against whom sufficient evidence for trial is lacking.
>
> Procedure: Suspect detainees may appear before the committee but do not have the right to demand such appearance. Due to the administrative nature and political mission of the PSC, procedures are far less exacting than those of the courts.
>
> Detention: Where evidence for trial is lacking, but it is apparent that the suspect is a threat to the national security, the committee may impose administrative ("an tri") detention. This is a type of preventative detention to protect the state from a known threat to its security. There is the additional provision of continual extension of two year terms if the individual remains a threat to the national security. "An Tri" detention is nonjudicial and administrative in nature. A violation of the national security laws need not be proven; all that must be demonstrated is that a reasonable belief exists that the suspect threatens the national security. Once "an tri" detention is imposed there are no judicial remedies. The duration and place of detention are governed by GVN administrative regulations.
>
> There is no rigid rule regarding the amount of evidence necessary for detention, and the criteria may vary significantly from province to province. Each committee determines the existing threat to national security based on conditions within the particular province, and the function of the detainee within the VCI. This process, because it is administrative and political in nature, reflects the political "facts-of-life" in the province.
>
> The PSC's are, by definition, political tools, and are governed from province to province by the political "facts-of-life." PSC existence is extra-constitutional and non-judicial, based upon the right of a State to survive.
>
> The nature of these committees, and their strictly political function, dictate a "hands-off" policy by all U.S. personnel and agencies. [15]

Between the military courts and the Provincial Security Committees, the government of south Viet Nam possesses the ability to imprison almost anyone it cares to. "Legal form, rarely observed with fidelity at any time in south Vietnam's recent history, has clearly been abandoned since the enemy offensive began...Although no government edict has been issued, the normal laws governing the rights of the accused appear to have been virtually suspended." [16]

SENTENCE REVIEW: Release or Renewal

When a person's sentence is completed there is no guarantee that he will be released from jail.

> --If a prisoner's file is lost, years of imprisonment and uncertainty are his fate.
>
> --The warden may be holding a prisoner in order to get a bribe from his family or friends. If they can't pay the prisoner is not released.

3-15 *Congressional Record*, April 22, 1971, pp. 3330-1

3-16 *New York Times*, August 13, 1972

--A prisoner may have been placed in administrative detention under the "an tri" law.
  His sentence can then be renewed indefinitely at the national government's discretion.

--The Ministry of Interior, which is in charge of reviewing sentences, can refuse to
  release a prisoner.

Take, for example, the case of Truong Van Bai. Bai was arrested in 1964 when he was an 18-year-old high school student participating in the anti-government student movement. He was sentenced to five years imprisonment.

He completed his sentence in September 1969. However, two years later he had not been released. Other prisoners who had seen him claimed that his legs were paralyzed from having been shackled for too long and that he was suffering from tuberculosis and liver disease.

In response to a letter from a relative asking that Bai be freed, the Ministry of Interior wrote on November 25, 1970:

"Responding to your letter dated July 15, 1970, asking to set free your brother Truong
Van Bai who was captured by the Thua Thien Security Agency in 1964, we solemnly inform
you that:

"Prisoner Truong Van Bai was accused of working for the Communists and was then sentenced
to 5 years imprisonment. During serving his sentence in Con Son, instead of repenting,
he showed his proof of opposition. Therefore, he should be detained a period of time
in addition.

"However, how long he should be detained depends on his level of repentence."

Prisoners who protest being held beyond their assigned sentences risk having those sentences extended or being subjected to immediate physical retaliation. Even the relatives of those in jail are careful not to register too vocal an objection for fear of police reprisals.

Years of experience with the injustices of the Saigon government have led to an attitude of sarcastic distain for its legal system. There is a street in downtown Saigon named "Cong Ly"--it literally means "justice." This street also happens to be one-way. So, the Vietnamese say, "In Viet Nam, justice is a one-way street."

Military Justice and Conscientious Objectors

In addition to national security cases involving civilians, the military courts deal with draft resistance and desertion. Though strictly classified as military, many of these cases actually relate to political issues.

South Viet Nam does not recognize religious or conscientious objection to war. Those who are opposed to killing fellow human beings for religious or ethical reasons are not exempt to the draft. Well over half of the population of Viet Nam adhere to Buddhism, which teaches non-violence and respect for every form of life. The ranks of the activist An Quang Pagoda Buddhists have been thoroughly and systematically thinned by the draft. The draft has also proven a highly efficient instrument of political repression against the high school and university student movements, which were the most consistent recent opponents of the war.

The U.S. government has been aware for years that the draft is a useful instrument of political control. A United States Army summary of south Vietnamese laws dated December 1967 points this out. "In lieu of making out a charge based on positive acts detrimental to the national security, or in addition thereto, the GVN is often able to charge and prove desertion from the armed forces, Draft Evasion, or the forging or use of False Identification documents or permits." [1]

The penalties for draft resistance are severe --solitary confinement and years of hard labor.

> Article 10: Are sentenced to solitary confinement with hard labor those youths:
>
> --Who use fraudulent manners or tricks so as to avoid presenting themselves when they reach the age to fulfill their military obligations.
>
> --Who make themselves physically disabled or ask other persons to cause their physical disability so as to avoid the fulfillment of their military obligations, either temporarily or permanently.
>
> The principal offender and his accomplices are sentenced to the same penalties.

(Decree Law 015/66)

The fate of those who are inducted into the army and later want to be discharged for conscientious reasons is even more harsh. Since they cannot apply for release on moral grounds, many desert. If apprehended, they are subject to being sent back to the front-line duty.

> Article 3: When serving their sentence, convicted deserters shall not be kept in jails but shall be sent directly to the field to serve in special Coolies of the Battlefield units.
>
> Article 4: Convicted deserters shall automatically receive the supplementary punishment of military degradation, be deprived of their rights to pay and allowances and in case of death shall be deprived of their rights to be recognized as having died for the country, and of the right to any subsidy of any kind for the widow, In case of wound or infirmity, they shall not be entitled to any subsidy or compensation-allowance.

(Decree-Law 015/66)

The coolies of the battlefield are the ammunition carriers on front lines; they are the servants for any soldier who wants an errand run. They are not allowed to carry guns and are the last to receive medical attention. If they die, their families are often not notified. No pension is paid to their wives and children if they are killed.

There are thousands now serving in these special units, many of whom are Buddhists and students with religious and political convictions against the war. They have been forced into the army. Though their plight does not show up in any of the official statistics, they are just as surely political prisoners as the inmates of Con Son.

---

[1] *Handbook on National Security: Laws and Procedures,* Saigon, December 1967

Prison Conditions

There are over two hundred national prisons and hundreds of local jails in south Viet Nam. A national prison is located in each province, most districts and all major cities, and there are five large national prisons at Chi Hoa, Tan Hiep, Thu Duc, Phu Quoc (for prisoners of war) and Con Son. A smaller national prison is located at the Cho Quan Hospital, where sick prisoners from the five large prisons and various interrogation centers are taken.

Provincial Prisons

Conditions vary greatly from prison to prison. In some provinces and districts where political activity is low and the director of the prison prohibits mistreatment of inmates, the only complaints are about overcrowding and poor food. This is an exception. In most provincial prisons, inhuman conditions and brutal treatment are commonplace.

Evidence of the prevalence of torture in a province prison has been discovered by medical personnel associated with the American Friends Service Committees (Quakers). For five years, they provided medical service for inmates of Quang Ngai Provincial Prison. What they found there was appalling. Testifying before a House Foreign Operations subcommittee on July 17, 1970, Marjorie Nelson, M.D., told of the overcrowding and inadequate conditions in the Quang Ngai jail.

> "I found the following: two small square rooms approximately 15 by 15 at most, with only small slit windows at the top of three walls, held respectively 50 and 40 women and children. No beds provided in either one.

> "A large room approximately 45 by 15, with two-tiered wooden bunks filling the room leaving an aisle between, housed 200 women. They sleep on the floor as well as on both tiers."

She added that prisoners were frequently removed from the jail and subjected to torture at the Province Interrogation Center.

> In her testimony Dr. Nelson said that during her weekly visits to the Quang Ngai Province Prison between September 1968 and September 1969, she saw dozens of patients who had coughed up, vomited or urinated blood after being beaten about the chest, back and stomach. On at least two occasions she was able to document by x-rays fractures of bones following beatings.

> Dr. Nelson, who speaks fluent Vietnamese and obtained all her information directly from patients, said that prisoners told her of being tortured by electricity, with wires attached to ears, nipples, and genitalia, by being forced to drink concoctions containing powdered lime and other noxious substances, by being tied up and suspended by ropes, often upside down.

> Dr. Nelson noted that on at least three occasions patients seriously ill or injured and under her care were removed to the Province Interrogation Center without her knowledge for further interrogation. [1]

A subsequent AFSC report indicates that the practice of torturing prisoners in the Interrogation Center continues.

> In August 1972, our workers in Quang Ngai observed several prisoners in the prison ward of the Quang Ngai Provincial Hospital after they had passed through a south Vietnamese interrogation center. A few of these cases illustrate the seriousness of the situation:

> A woman prisoner was subject to continual seizures. After interrogation and beating to the point of unconsciousness, she complained of vaginal bleeding and an examination was performed. In the prison ward she had as many as ten seizures a night. Further examination showed swelling on her head which she said resulted from the police banging her head against a wall. An X-ray confirmed a skull fracture with resulting paralysis to the right side of her body.

[1] News Release, American Friends Service Committee, July 23, 1970

A 17-year old boy, near death, had been unable to urinate for four days and was in extreme pain. After treatment by a Quaker docter, we were informed that the prisoner had been tortured by electric charges to his genital organs.

A young girl had seizures, stared into space and exhibited symptoms of loss of memory. She said she had been forced to drink a lime solution many times while being inter-rogated.

Another girl told us she had been forced to drink a lime-filled whitewash solution after which guards had jumped on her bloated stomach. She said she had also been beaten with a heavy club. She complained of pain in the chest and stomach and was observed having seizures.

Two women were chained together in the prison ward. One, 45, had chest pains and said she had been subjected to electric torture. She also had seizures so violent that they caused the hospital bed to move several feet. The other woman who was older, said she had been beaten with a club on chest, neck and face. The Quaker doctor examined her and found her face severely swollen, her chest and neck bruised and a chest X-ray showed cracked ribs. She also said she had been forced to drink a lime solution. [2]

Conditions in other south Vietnamese prisons do not differ substantially from those at Quang Ngai. Doug Hostetter, who spent three years in Viet Nam with Viet Nam Christian Service offers a comprehensive look at what life is like in Quang Tri Provincial Prison.

From July 1966, until June 1969, I lived and worked in community development in the village of Tam Ky, south Viet Nam, about 40 miles south of Da Nang. For almost 2 years I conducted tailoring and literacy classes in the Quang Tin Province prison located in Tam Ky. ... In spite of the overcrowded housing, poor food and use of torture in the provincial prison, accommodations there were considered a luxury when compared to the infamous Con Son prison on Devil's Island...

The prisoners fall roughly into three categories: common villagers from hamlets under areas controlled by the NLF, non-communist political prisoners, and actual NLF officials or guerillas. From the prisoners I talked to I would estimate that about five per cent of the prison population were NLF officials and guerillas who were taken prisoner in battle, infiltrators discovered in the Saigon Government, or NLF party officials captured by Vietnamese police or agents of the Phoenix program. This group of prisoners were to have been sent to Con Son prison island, but bribes paid to the warden kept them in the provincial prison.

I would estimate that between 70 and 80% of the prisoners would fall into the category of more or less innocent bystanders who happened to live in the wrong village. These prisoners are guilty not for anything that they did or even believed, but because of where they lived....The third category which I have called the non-communist political prisoners made up about 10 or 20% of the prisoners. The prisoners in this category are almost entirely Buddhists. According to the south Vietnamese constitution it is illegal to be pro-communist or to be neutralist. ...Anyone who advocates peace, or a coalition government is of course also neutralist and can be arrested. Prisoners in this category are Buddhist monks, members of the Unified Buddhist Church who have been active in working for peace or coalition government, members of various peace groups, members of political parties which do not support the Thieu, Ky regime, and students, workers or peasants who protest against the war or the Saigon government.....

Later in 1969, in another survey I attempted to discover how many children were being held prisoner in the Quang Tin Prison. It would appear that being a VC is hereditary; if the parents are "VC" the children are considered to be "VC" also. On May 17, 1965, the date of the survey of the Quang Tin Provincial Prison, there were 60 VC suspects under 11 years old. They fall into the following age categories: two "VC" age one or below, 14 age two, 9 age three, 6 age four, 13 age five, 9 age seven, 4 age eight, and 3 age 10.

[5-2] News Release, American Friends Service Committee, October 31, 1972

Earlier when I had noticed the children I had assumed that the children were not really prisoners, but just came along when their parents were arrested. Experience proved that this assumption was wrong. In October 1968, I was in one of the rooms where the women and children are kept when I noticed a small boy about 6 years old who had a large boil on his stomach which badly needed medical attention. When I asked for the child's mother I was told that his mother had caught malaria while in prison and had been taken to the provincial hospital. The child was at that time being cared for by his 10 year old sister who also looked after another 4 year old brother. When I requested permission to take the three children to the hospital, the warden said that it would not be possible. When I became angry and insisted, the warden said that they could go only if they were accompanied by a prison guard (to assure that the 10, 6, and 4 year old VC did not escape). The children were left at the hospital with their mother so that all could be treated together. When the mother died of malaria the following week, we had the children sent immediately to an orphanage. Upon discovering this, the prison officials were furious. They accused me of helping three prisoners to escape. [3]

National Prisons

Conditions in provincial jails are deplorable, but conditions in the large national prisons are consistently worse. [4] Letters smuggled out of these jails detail a number of abuses which are familiar to inmates of all the national prisons.

Food

The life of the prisoners at Con Son is miserable. A handful of rice with some sauce full of sand and pebbles and rotten fish...The ration for one person is given to five. We were given three meals with seven hours and then we had to wait for seventeen hours without any food. We were given vegetables only four times in eight months. Only once were we given fresh rau muong (a leafy vegetable similar to spinach) which the Vietnamese never eat raw. These were given to us after terrible beatings by the "criminals" Ve and Tran. Now the women have no vegetables to eat.

We were not given enough food and drink. If we asked for more they sometimes answered us by mixing our rice with petroleum, or mixing our dried rotten fish with soap, or giving us uncooked rice. We had stomach aches from these foods and when we were sick, they refused to give us rice soup. We denounced this to the nurses. When they were in a good mood they gave us some grains of salt for our rice soup. When not, we had to eat plain rice soup. Often they did not allow us to wash our bowls. So we had to eat out of dirty bowls on which the flies, dogs and poultry stepped, or mice ran over. Rice was usually mixed with dust, the kind of dust that comes from the outdoor toilets through gusts of wind. We asked for clean bowls to eat out of. They hurried us. ."If you eat slowly, we'll dump all your rice in one bowl and you'll have to eat like dogs from one bowl." Some women were sick and could not eat. They wanted to save their food, but their bowls were grabbed and the rice thrown away. "Next time, watch out," they were told.

In addition, the food provided prisoners is insufficient and particularly bad. Their food intake for a meal is just five (5) piastres. This includes rice and other food. Each prisoner of ordinary crimes is supposedly offered 50 grams of fish and 50 grams of vegetables, but actually he has never been provided with the whole of his portion. His rice is always half-cooked, mixed with ashes and dirt. For other food, he gets ill-smelling ready-boiled fish and some wilted vegetables which have turned yellow.

[5-3] *South Vietnamese Prisons,* Report by Doug Hostetter, June 1969

[5-4] "An opposition deputy of South Vietnam's lower house has charged that political and criminal prisoners were dying in the country's jails because of poor food and lack of medicine. In an open letter to Prime Minister Tran Thien Khiem, deputy Ho Ngoc Nhuan said the government was spending only about 12 cents a day on food and medicine for each prisoner." *Washington Post,* December 21, 1972.

Each room of more than one hundred prisoners is given 36 kilograms of ready-cooked rice and about 30 grams of vegetables and fish a day. [5]

Prison Conditions

[The cells on Con Son Island]

This is a room, or more correctly a small cage about 3 meters (10 feet) long and 1 1/2 meters (5 feet) wide, in an area separated from the other cages by many walls and totally isolated from all life outside. They threw five people into this narrow cage. On the average, each person had only about 2 hand-breadths of space in which to lie and live. The legs were shackled and held high day and night--even while eating, sleeping, washing--fastened to a metal rod. They forced us to lie in silence; we couldn't sit or stir in this hot, narrow, dark cage. The cages are separated by stone walls more than a meter thick. A small door is kept shut tightly all day, except for a few minutes when it is opened and reclosed during meals. Above it are metal bars running horizontally lengthwise, with a small space or passageway left for the orderlies who make regular checks. We had to lie there all day. Sitting or standing (during the first months) was not allowed. We had only to murmer one or two words ever so softly under our breath and we had to pay for it with the cruel lashings of the orderlies, as ordered by the Administration of the prison. Even when the latrine barrel was open and leaking all over so the floor had a pasty covering, we still had to lie quietly and endure it. The tile roof had leaked for years and never been repaired, and during the rains the water poured down into the cage, not to mention the sand pebbles and blinding dust that came in on windy days. The ground where we lay was uneven, rough, bumpy with sand, pebbles and dirt since it was many years since the last time it had been cleaned. We were kept here continuously for the first four months. They throw girls and women prisoners into these places. [6]

Mistreatment and Torture

[Huyen Tan] Mam, President of the Saigon University Student Association and President of the National Student Union of south Viet Nam, was arrested for the third time last January 5, a few days after he published a statement against U.S. bombing of north Viet Nam. His 65-year-old mother paid many visits to the National Police Headquarters to inquire about him, and was repeatedly told that he had not been arrested--a very usual answer. On March 14, a student friend noticed, on the office wall of the Headquarters, a list of prisoners transferred back there from the Joint U.S.-Vietnamese Intelligence Center. Mam's name was on it. Another student had earlier seen him transferred in late February from the Headquarters to the Center, lying all bloody on a stretcher. Finally, and without any explanation, the police admitted on April 4 to his mother that he was being held at the National Police Headquarters.

At about the same time, a high school student happened to see Mam there. Mam's face was so swollen and peeling that had Mam not called him over, he would not have recognized him. Mam told him that his condition resulted from being subjected to the glare of 200-watt light bulbs placed directly in front of his eyes. The lights were left on for two hours at a time, or until his skin started to burn and blister. The lights would then be turned off for about twenty minutes and then turned on again. He said this happened several times a day for a period of 20 days. Mam had also been badly beaten on his legs and knees and that he was unable to walk. He had in addition been tortured with electric shocks to his fingers and earlobes and by having his fingers tied together, a ruler placed in between them and twisted. [7]

5-5 *A Denouncement of the Crimes Committed by the Wardens of Chi Hoa and Con Son Prisons,* A signed report smuggled out of Chi Hoa Prison, Autumn 1972, p.4.

5-6 *Report of Five Students Released from Con Son Island,* May 25, 1970, p.3.

5-7 Statement of Nguyen Tang Huyen, June 30, 1972. (Based on reports smuggled out of jail) p. 4.

Another description of torture in prisons was supplied by women who were confined in Con Son.

> When the women cried out when they heard cries of protest coming from the men's tiger
> cages, Nhan and Sum, shirtless, shouted: "I give orders to throw lime on them until
> they die." The trustees rushed towards us, throwing bags and buckets of lime upon us
> which had been set on the iron bars above. Buckets of water followed. We were choked
> and burned by the lime mixed with the water. Many fainted, others vomited blood. One
> woman was seriously injured when a block of hard lime fell upon her head. At the
> same time they went into the dispensary and threw lime onto the patients four times
> until all of them collapsed. Despite that, they stuck the rest of the lime into the
> nose, mouth and eyes of the patients so that some were blinded, others vomited and
> coughed out blood. After the repression, our bodies as well as our belongings were
> all covered with lime. Yet they did not allow us to wash ourselves and clean the cells.
> So for two months, we kept lying in the lime...[8]

Prisoner of War Camps

Prison camps which hold captured north Vietnamese and National Liberation Front soldiers (as distinguished
from NLF political personnel) have received considerable publicity from south Vietnamese and American
officials.

The International Red Cross is authorized to visit POW camps and has been allowed into those run by Saigon.
Their official reports have been generally favorable, but an accurate assessment is simply impossible on
a brief guided visit by prison authorities. Independent reports tell of less than adequate conditions.

> Phuquoc is an island off the south Vietnamese coast near Cambodia. The prison camp
> currently houses about 40,000 men, most Viet Cong but also some north Vietnamese.

> A woodcutter interviewed in a fishing village about a mile from the camp said the
> prisoners "go on strike quite often. They beat the tin walls of their barracks with
> rice bowls. It would like 10 jet planes taking off."

> The owner of a fish sauce factory said, "The prisoners are dissatisfied with their
> food. The Americans set high standards all right, but they are not met." A bystander
> added that the prisoners are fed only the cheapest fish, a small body species called
> liet. "Sometimes they refuse to accept the food because it is so poor. They say the
> fish is on occasion even rotten."

> The food is supplied to the camp by a Saigon contractor. "Many contractors bid for
> the contract, so the price is very low," one local resident said.

> Last week seven prisoners attempted an escape by tunneling out. Four succeeded but
> the other three were recaptured and shot, [emphasis added] according to a soldier in
> the island security force.[9]

Apparently there is much that the Red Cross has missed. It is no wonder that reporters are barred from
admittance into the Prisoner of War camps.

The Red Cross is permitted to inspect only those facilities which hold inmates protected by the Geneva
Conventions—a small percentage of the total prisoner population of south Viet Nam. Each Red Cross visit is
announced well ahead of time to the prison administrators. Under these circumstances, few violations are
recorded. Penal officials regularly conceal maltreatment of prisoners, as these personal accounts show.

> He, (Mr. Dan, a guard in the south Vietnamese prison system) said that an International
> Red Cross team toured the compound shortly after the escape, but they did not see the
> dying, recaptured men. Dan reported that those men had been carried in knee-high,
> portable cages to the nearby jungle and hidden until after the Red Cross departed to
> make its favorable report on prison conditions.[10]

5-8 *A Denouncement*, p. 8

5-9 *Washington Post*, June 8, 1972

5-10 *Pacific News Service*, John Champlin, M. D.

A former inmate of Con Son reports a similar experience.

"Did groups ever come to visit the prison?"

"Yes," he told me. "When the Americans came, the guards locked the doors. I wanted to see them but I couldn't."

"They never let the delegations see the old men or the sick," another claimed. "They would be taken up to the mountain before the group of visitors would arrive. When the Red Cross delegation came, all those who spoke English were taken away." [11]

An American interrogator who worked at the Saigon Military Interrogation Center reported:

When the Red Cross delegation visits the center, the authorities are given one week's notice, and on the day of the visit, the prisoners receive an extra meal and more food at each meal." [12]

Despite these actions by south Vietnamese prison officials, the Red Cross has nevertheless filed a number of reports critical of conditions in south Vietnamese prisons.

According to informed sources, Red Cross representatives have recorded numerous complaints from prisoners at the camp on Phu Quoc island, charging prison guards with brutality and protesting inadequate housing, medical facilities, and food... The latest report was based on a Red Cross visit to the island two weeks ago. [13]

Mr. Daniel of the International Red Cross said on May 26, 1971:

Where we need to go the most is where we aren't allowed.

U.S. government photo showing NLF prisoners being paraded through the streets of Quang Ngai. Sign around the woman's neck reads: "Here is a wicked communist for you to see." Article 13 of the Geneva Conventions Relative to the Treatment of Prisoners of War states: "Prisoners of war must at all times be protected, particularly against acts of violence or intimidation and against insults and public curiosity.

5-11Interview by Don Luce with inmates just released from Con Son Prison

5-12*Dispatch News Service,* April 27, 1971

5-13*Christian Science Monitor,* November 2, 1970

American Prisoners of War

On December 2, 1972, the Pentagon listed 469 Americans as prisoners of war and 438 as missing in action in north Viet Nam. On September 29, 1972, the north Vietnamese listed 385 men captured. According to the Committee of Liaison with Families of Servicemen Detained in North Viet Nam, just prior to the 469 figure, the Pentagon reclassified several men from the missing in action list to the POW list without confirmation from the north Vietnamese.

There are many people better qualified to discuss the issue of U.S. captured pilots and other soldiers captured in the war than the authors of this study. We can add some specific information on eight U.S. captured pilots that one of us visited in Hanoi on October 30, 1972.

The men lived in what appeared to be an old French villa. They had three bedrooms for the eight men. In one room there was a guitar; in another, a goldfish bowl with four goldfish. All of the men appeared to be in excellent health, both physically and mentally.

Capt. William Bryns of Warrenton, Missouri described a typical day in the prison:

> "We get up at about 6:30 and sometimes quarter to seven and we have a breakfast meal which consists of warm milk and bread. We get two loaves of French style bread. It's a small loaf about this big and that big around which is plenty   Then we do personal hygiene, brush our teeth and clean up. We clean up our rooms and the courtyard. Then maybe we'll have volleyball or work in the garden or something like that--some kind of exercise in the morning. Then we have a lunch meal which is soup and some kind of side dish, soybean curd, some kind of meat, fish, or something like this. Then we have rest time. Some kind of custom I guess. Then we come out in the afternoon and do some kind of activity. We're allowed outside freely. We take a bath everyday. Then we have an afternoon meal--soup and a sidedish. Of course we have our bread. Then we go in for the evening and we have Voice of Viet Nam and Camp radio. Camp radio has some kind of program with American music. We usually play cards in the evening."

Vietnamese villagers in north Viet Nam have been instructed to give good care to captured U.S. pilots. Quang Ba village, 15 miles out of Hanoi, has a special medical kit in case a pilot is captured. There are splints for broken bones, the fuzz of a local plant that stops bleeding, bandages and iodine.

(Photo by Don Luce)

Five of the eight captured U.S. pilots visited on October 30, 1972. They are, from left to right: Major James Padgett of Mattydale, N.Y., Navy Lt. Tom Latendresse of La Moore, Cal,, Capt. William Bryns of Warrenton, Mo., Capt. Ray Bean of Littleton, Col., and Navy Lt. Albert Molinare of San Diego, Cal.

Navy Lt. Tom Latendresse of Le Moore, California described his treatment this way:

> My aircraft got hit and was uncontrollable and I punched out. I hit the ground within ten seconds. I had a broken leg, I believe--[at least] an injured leg and an injured arm. Pretty bad I thought. I hurt and smarted. I couldn't move and within ten minutes there were local people around me and local militia. They immediately transported me to what I would call a field hospital and treated my wounds. They did a right fine job. Then I was transported up to Hanoi. I ran across Bill [Byrns] and Ray [Bean] here about half-way up and I got good care on the way up. As a matter of fact it was a bumpy ride. They made me a bed of palm leaves. I got to Hanoi and they took me to the hospital here in Hanoi and worked on me and as you can see I'm in good shape now."

The villagers of Quang Ba once shot down an American F-105. The pilot, they said, "flew down by parachute and was immediately captured."

"He was captured," the village chief said, "but no one beat him. He was given food and water, then turned over to the government."

When asked what the pilot looked like, the chief replied, "he was big," and added: "he looked like the pictures of all the Americans we've seen in the papers."

When they were bombing north Viet Nam, the pilots said they had been told that the reason for the bombing was to get the POWs released. Now that they are prisoners, they disagree with this. Capt. Byrns explained why:

> "One thing we were told before we got shot down was we were bombing to help get the prisoners back and that sounded like a pretty good cause. But now I realize, and I wish you'd tell the American people this, that prisoners do not jump for joy when we have an air raid around here. We had bombs come pretty close to the camp one day. The only jumping we do is down on the floor and cover up our heads. We're probably safe because we're protected by the Vietnamese people. They put us in our rooms and they close the windows, the shutters and protect us as much as they can. But the point is, we're not jumping for joy over it. We'd like to see it ended so that we can go home."

The medic at Quang Ba village with his special kit to give first aid attention to wounded U.S. pilots.

(Photo by Don Luce)

21

U. S. Government caption : "Youthful hard-core Viet Cong,
heavily guarded, awaits interrogation..."

The Phoenix Program

The Phung Hoang or Phoenix Program was originally designed by the United States to "neutralize"[1] the political apparatus of the National Liberation Front or VCI (Viet Cong Infrastructure). The techniques used range from paying informers to assassination. Though generally conceded to be a failure in terms of reducing the NLF's political strength, the Phoenix program has come to be a significant aspect in the repression of political dissent in south Viet Nam.

Wayne Cooper, a former Foreign Service Officer who spent most of his 18 months in Viet Nam as an advisor to the Phoenix Program described the origins of the operation:

> In the mid 1960's, the Central Intelligence Agency began a program which came to be known as "counter terror" or "C.T." It was a unilateral American program, never recognized by the south Vietnamese government. CIA representatives recruited, organized, supplied and directly paid CT teams, whose function was to use Viet Cong techniques of terror—assassination, abuses, kidnappings and intimidation—against the Viet Cong leadership. [2]

Cooper traces the development of the Phoenix Program from an exclusively American operation to its incorporation into the Saigon police network. In the process, the original objectives of Phoenix were altered.

> In the field, we saw the inertia and ineptitude and knew the program wasn't succeeding. But we failed to notice that Phung Hoang was becoming something else—a means for repressive political control over the south Vietnamese. ...The "subversive" nationalist who expressed fatigue with the war, scorn for Thieu and Ky, and enthusiasm for a coalition government, was by definition a threat to public security. He might easily find himself on Con Son Island, his arrest being explained to advisors by ascribing to him a VCI title. [3]

PHOENIX TODAY

Members of the VCI are considered neutralized if they: voluntarily surrender or "rally" to the Saigon government; are killed; or are imprisoned or detained. The ralliers become the responsibility of the Chieu Hoi (Open Arms) Program, which aims to "reeducate" former NLF followers to become loyal citizens of south Viet Nam. Returnees who do not become reeducated are sent to jail; those who complete the Chieu Hoi Program are eligible for the draft.

The south Vietnamese government claims that most of those killed under Phoenix die in fire fights with Saigon or paramilitary police forces. How many people are actually assassinated is unknown, because the Phoenix program has tried to shed its counter-terror image, as it moved into the open as part of a pacification program. In spite of this, it is certain that a number of those listed as killed have died as a result of torture administered while they were being interrogated or detained. In hearings before the House Foreign Affairs Committee, K. Barton Osborn, a former intelligence operative in Viet Nam, testified on specific instances.

7-1 "Another CORDS Phoenix advisor enlightened me on the word 'neutralization.' Previously, he explained, the major goal of Phoenix was the 'elimination' of the VCI. 'Elimination,' however, gave the unfortunate impression to some Congressmen and to the interested public that someone was being 'eliminated.' Now the major goal is 'neutralization' of the VCI. Of course, the same proportion of VCI are being killed in combat, and killed or captured by the mobile teams established for that purpose. But Congress seems mollified now that suspected Vietcong are 'neutralized ' rather than 'eliminated'." Statement of Richard Winslow, former AID employee, to Government Operations Subcommittee *U.S. Assistance Programs in Vietnam,* July 21, 1971, p.24.

7-2 Wayne Cooper, "Operation Phoenix: A Vietnam Fiasco Seen From Within," *Washington Post,* June 8, 1972

7-3 *Ibid.*

They antagonized him several times by taking him with his elbows behind his back, hands tied, running him up to the door of the helicopter and saying: "If you don't tell us what we need to know we are going to throw you out of the helicopter." They did this two or three times and he refused to say anything. He couldn't respond. He wouldn't respond. Therefore, on the fourth trip to the door they did throw him out from the helicopter to the ground.

I saw other interrogations, to describe them briefly: The use of the insertion of the 6-inch dowel into the 6-inch canal of one of my detainee's ears and the tapping through the brain until he dies. The starving to death of a Vietnamese woman who was suspected of being part of the local political education cadre in one of the local villages. They simply starved her to death in a cage that they kept in one of the hooches at that very counterintelligence team headquarters. [4]

Osborn also stated that:

I will say this: individually I never knew an individual to be detained as a VC suspect who ever lived through an interrogation in a year and a half, and that included quite a number of individuals. That may be my experience; may be a tremendous exception to the rule, but the experience of my peers there and my own experience firsthand, which I swear to, and have sworn to, was categorically inhuman and with no rhyme, reason or bureaucratic justification for a murder program which had gone way beyond the level of any competence at that level. [5]

The "captured" are apprehended by military or police units and eventually confront the judicial system. These suspects encounter the worst aspects of Vietnamese "justice" including arbitrary arrest, torture, no trial and renewable two-year sentences. A vast number of those currently held by the south Vietnamese government have been apprehended under Operation Phoenix.

The plight of those captured under the Phoenix Program can be best understood by placing oneself in the position of a prospective victim.

--He is apprehended either by a military unit sweeping through his town or village by the Special Branch of the National Police.

--He may be on a district or provincial police "blacklist" of security suspects because of reports by paid informers or his fellow villagers. Informers often turn people in simply to earn a fee, and neighbors use this as a convenient way to settle a grudge.

--Once detained, a suspect has no legal rights. Habeus Corpus was suspended over 5 years ago and the police can hold arrestees up to 46 days for investigation. During this time, suspects are often tortured to obtain confessions, which are admissable as evidence.

--If sufficient evidence is gathered to warrant a trial, the suspect goes before a military court. He has no right of appeal unless a death penalty is imposed.

--If there is not enough evidence for a trial, the accused is brought before a Provincial Security Committee and may be detained for up to two years--and his sentence is renewable.

An examination of testimony presented before Congress and of official Phoenix documents reveals that these abuses of justice are not accidental but an integral part of the Phoenix Program.

Theoretically, those captured by Phoenix are high-level local VCI, identified by means of carefully screened information from paid informers and the local populace. In fact, evidence from these sources has often proved unreliable. As Michael Uhe, a former military intelligence officer testified:

7-4 *Twenty-Second Report by the Committee on Government Operations,* October 17, 1972, p. 100

7-5 *Ibid,* p. 101

Our paid sources could easily have been either provocateurs or opportunists
with a score to settle. Every information report (IR) we wrote based on our sources'
information was classified; (1) unverifiable and (2) usually reliable source. As to
the first, it speaks for itself; the second, in most cases was pure rationale for the
existence of the program. [6]

Information is also to be obtained from the general population. The instructions on who should be reported
are not a model of legal precision. For example, a document distributed in Viet Nam to United States
advisors to Phoenix describes the type of actions reported by neighbors which could get a person blacklisted.

Residents of the area who make suspicious utterances, such as, (1) expressions which
distort Government of Vietnam policies and the action of Government of Vietnam cadres;
(2) false rumors which confuse and frighten the people; (3) creation of division and
and hatred among the populace and between the populace and the Government of Vietnam
cadres.

Those who act suspiciously:

(a) the hesitation or fearful attitude of a dishonest person;
(b) contact with those whom we suspect; or
(c) regular secret colloquies of a certain group of people in the area. [7]

Predictably, these methods of soliciting information have proven totally inadequate. The number of people
falsely killed or imprisoned is unknown--but the following dialogue between U.S. Ambassador to south Viet Nam,
William Colby, and Congressman Ogden Reid of New York gives some idea of the margin of error.

Mr. Reid: Can you say there is a high degree of accuracy in the initial dossier or report
or report or do you have some concern as to the accuracy?
Ambassador Colby: I have never been highly satisfied with the accuracies of our
intelligence effort on the Vietcong Infrastructure.
Mr. Reid: Are we talking about substantial number, say over a thousand, who might
have been improperly identified, or are you talking in terms of a hundred or what?
Ambassador Colby: I would say initially identified, misidentified. I would say that
in the past you had larger numbers than that.
Mr. Reid: Meaning what, over 5,000?
Ambassador Colby: I wouldn't like to give you a figure, but I would say that--
Mr. Reid: Or 7,000? Is that the implication?
Ambassador Colby: I frankly don't have a number, Mr. Congressman. [8]

Suspects picked up under the Phoenix program have to endure two months in an interrogation center before being
sentenced. Police officials frequently torture these citizens during this period. The widespread use of
torture during interrogation can be explained by the admissability of confession as evidence in court and by
the fact that local officials are under pressure from Saigon to sentence a specified number of high level NLF
officials each month.

According to Ambassador Colby, Phoenix divides the VCI into three categories; A leaders, B cadre and
C followers. "The goals assigned to the provinces and districts apply only to those A and B category
personnel and only to those actually sentenced rather than merely captured." [9]

If a district or province chief cannot identify and arrest VCI members by means of informants, he produces
his assigned quota by torturing confessions out of the suspects he has on hand. Michael Uhl observed the
impact of this quota system while working as an intelligence officer in Viet Nam.

For instance, Ambassador Colby gave the impression that Phoenix targeted specific
high level Vietcong Infrastructure whose identity had been established by at least
three unrelated intelligence sources. In his prepared statement delivered before
this committee on July 19, 1971, he cites several interesting statistics. Among

[7-6] *Ibid*, p. 52

[7-7] Excerpt from Phoenix document "Analysis of Provincial Security Committees (SOP-3)", *Ibid, p. 98*

[7-8] *Ibid*. p. 48

[7-9] *Ibid*. p. 49

these is the number of Vietcong Infrastructure (VCI) successfully targeted and
"neutralized" during the period 1968-May 1971. 1970 figures show 22,341 Vietcong
Infrastructure 'neutralized." Colby thus would have us believe that the vast
majority of these people were targeted according to the rules that he outlined.

This capacity on the part of military intelligence groups in Vietnam seems to me
greatly exaggerated. A mammoth task such as this would greatly tax even our
resourceful FBI, where we have none of the vast cross-cultural problems to contend
with.

What types of operations "generate" this supplementary body count then, assuming
the figures are accurate? It was my experience that the majority of people class-
fied as Vietcong Infrastructure were "captured" as a result of sweeping tactical
operations. In effect, a huge dragnet was cast out in our area of operation (AR) and
whatever looked good in the catch, regardless of evidence, was classified as
Vietcong Infrastructure.

Uhl went on to tell the subcommittee:

All CD's, because of this command pressure (the majority of our detaines were
classified as CD's), were listed as Vietcong Infrastructure. To my knowledge,
not one of these people ever freely admitted being a cadre member. And again,
contrary to Colby's statement, most of our CD's were women and children. [10]

After interrogation and investigation, the suspect encounters the sentencing stage of Phoenix. He is either
brought before a military court or a Provincial Security Committee, depending on whether there is sufficient
evidence for trial. (See Chapter 3, The Process of Justice, and etc. for procedures and sentencing.) From
either group, the suspect usually ends up with a sentence of several years in prison and there is no appeal.

Those who have been unlucky enough to be apprehended under Phoenix are never confronted with the evidence
against them or allowed legal council. They have entered a process where conviction is almost a certainty.
Every step of the way there is pressure to elevate a mere suspect to the A or B categories. The abuses of
this program are obvious. As the Committee on Government Operations concluded in the summer of 1971:

The committee notes that, according to official figures furnished by Ambassador Colby,
a total of 20,587 suspected VCI were killed from the beginning of 1968 through May
1971. It is impossible not to wonder how many of those persons were the innocent
victims of faulty intelligence. The committee can think of no other U.S.-funded or
supported program in which the consequences of inefficient management are so extreme. [11]

Despite its appearance as a totally Vietnamese operation, the Phoenix Program is actually a microcosm of the
profound U.S. influence which permeates the affairs of the south Vietnamese people. While few Americans
are directly involved in the program, Phoenix was created, organized and funded by the CIA. The district
and provincial interrogation centers were constructed with American funds and provided with American advisors.
Quotas were set by Americans. The national system of identifying suspects was devised by Americans and
underwritten by the United States. Informers are paid with U.S. funds. American tax dollars have covered
the expansion of the police and paramilitary units who arrest suspects.

The Phoenix Program is still funded entirely by the United States [12] and American advisors continue working
with the police, the courts and the interrogation centers of Phoenix.

The Phoenix or Phung Hoang Program was named after an all-seeing mythical bird which selectively snatches
its prey--but the techniques of this operation are anything but selective. For many Vietnamese, the Phung
Hoang Program is a constant menace to their lives. The New York Times recently entitled an article on the
program, "The Phoenix is a Bird of Death."

7-10 Ibid. p. 51

7-11 Ibid. p. 54

7-12 Ibid. p. 98

American Responsibility and the Saigon Government

The government of President Nguyen Van Thieu is a narrowly-based, military regime. It has been described by the pro-government Saigon Daily News as "a coalition of the extreme right."[1]   It is opposed by the National Liberation Front--and it is also opposed by the majority of the most politically active Buddhist and Catholic clergy, labor leaders, students and intellectuals. The military result of this opposition has been a devastating war; the political result has been a vast apparatus of repression.

United States funding and advising of the prison and police systems of south Viet Nam make us responsible for the current plight of the political prisoners. In a larger sense, the U.S. must share responsibility for the nature of the Saigon government itself. It is a government of limited scope whose very essence is dictated by American policy, not Vietnamese reality.

The Pentagon Papers record the objectives and the difficulties of American efforts in Indochina. From the very beginning, the United States faced almost insurmountable obstacles in establishing a pro-American government in Viet Nam. In 1948, the State Department asserted that Ho Chi Minh "probably is now supported by a considerable majority of the Vietnamese people ...[and] is the strongest and perhaps the ablest figure in Indochina and that any suggested solution which excludes him is an expedient of uncertain outcome."[2]

In spite of this fact, the effort to find a rival to Ho continued and the Catholic mandarin, Ngo Dinh Diem was selected. The American objective was a strong anti-communist government.[3]   The problem with the plan was that in the eyes of most of the people of south Viet Nam, the Viet Minh were the nationalists,[4] and Diem "existed by reason of U.S. support."[5]

As the nationwide election set for the summer of 1956 by the Geneva Conference approached, Diem's chances of winning did not improve. But rather than allow the Vietnamese to elect a communist, whether nationalist or not, the United States and Diem cancelled the scheduled election.[6]   The cancellation of elections had an immediate political impact in south Viet Nam. The very month of the scheduled election, the CIA declared "The trend toward authoritarian rule through the political parties led by Diem's relatives and a small circle of trusted associates will probably continue. Isolation and neutralization of government critics and men disliked or distrusted by Diem will also continue."[7]

The United States continued to support Diem despite increasing repression. By 1959, the political situation had become very uneasy. "This dissatisfaction is caused primarily by the authoritarian and pervasive political

[8-1]*Saigon Daily News*, May 29, 1969

[8-2]State Department Policy Statement on Indochina, September 27, 1948. (GPO 8, pp. 145 - 48) [Footnotes which which cite the *Pentagon Papers* will use the following abbreviations in referring to different editions of the Papers. BEA means Beacon Press, and GPO stands for Government Printing Office. Both abbreviations are then followed by the volume number and the page number.]

[8-3]" In French - U.S. discussion here, we and French have reached conclusion we should support Diem in establishment and maintenance of a strong, anti-communist national government." State Department Telegram, September 30, 1954 (GPO 10, p. 765)

[8-4]"Furthermore, nationalist appeal in Viet Nam is so closely identified with Ho Chi Minh and the Viet Min Minh movement that, even in areas outside Communist control, candidates and issues connected with 'nationali 'nationalism' and supported by the Viet Minh would probably be supported by a majority of the people." International Security Agency to State Department, April 22, 1955 (GPO 10, p. 935-36)

[8-5]John Foster Dulles' Telegram to Saigon Embassy, April 9, 1955 (GPO 10, p. 908)

[8-6]"Only the U.S. presence held the south together under far more favorable circumstances, and enabled Diem to refuse to go through with the 1954 provision calling for nationwide 'free' elections in 1956." Defense Secretary Robert McNamara, Memorandum for President Jonhson, March 16, 1964 (BEA III,p. 503)

[8-7]CIA National Intelligence Estimate, July 1956 (GPO 10, p.1080)

controls of the Ngo (Dinh Diem) family and its associates." [8]   U.S. officials, while making no public admissions, were well aware of Diem's activities. One such official, General Edward G. Lansdale, commented privately, "I cannot truly sympathize with Americans who help promote a fascistic state and then get angry when it doesn't act like a democracy." [9]

This first American experiment at creating an anti-communist government for the Vietnamese ended with the assassination of President Diem on November 1, 1963. Months of civil turmoil preceded this event and by the fall of 1963, even the United States had been forced to admit its error. Representatives of the U.S. military and the CIA played a major role in the coup which brought Diem down.

But the U.S. government still persisted in its efforts to dictate a type of government for south Viet Nam. No political accommodation was to be allowed. President Johnson wrote the U.S. Ambassador to Saigon: "It ought to be possible to explain in Saigon that your mission is precisely for the purpose of knocking down the idea of neutralization wherever it rears its ugly head, and on this point I think that nothing is more important than to stop the neutralist talk wherever we can and by whatever means we can." [10]

The political chaos which followed Diem's overthrow continued for 18 months and ended with a military coup led by Nguyen Cao Ky and Nguyen Van Thieu. They supported U.S. objectives--and reinstituted political controls which had characterized Diem era.

To preserve this pro-American government the United States mounted a dual effort. To counter NLF insurgency, half a million men and a vast arsenal of supplies were sent to Indochina; to control the political opposition in south Viet Nam, millions of dollars and hundreds of advisors were dispatched to organize the national police system. American troops apprehended thousands of Vietnamese civilians. They were turned over to the south Vietnamese National Police whose salaries were paid for by U.S. tax dollars and who were trained and advised by Americans. Suspects then were detained, interrogated and often tortured in U.S.-financed centers. After sentencing, they were imprisoned in jails expanded and outfitted by U.S. agencies. Except that U.S. troops arrest fewer Vietnamese, this picture remains the same today.

The United States has claimed that the repression of political opposition and treatment of prisoners are internal affairs of south Viet Nam. But such an opinion indicates how limited the U.S.'s view of Vietnamese sovereignty really is. We created the Diem government, then deposed it; we sent half a million troops, then withdrew them. We bombed their land and defoliated their forests without asking permission--and yet in deference to their independence we permit them to abuse their prisoners.

[8-8]Operations Coordinating Board, January 7, 1959 (GPO 10, p. 1166)

[8-9]Letter to Secretary of Defense, January 17, 1961 (GPO II, p. 9)

[8-10]Letter to Henry Cabot Lodge, March 20, 1964, (BEA III, p. 511)

Con Son—A Personal View

In 1966, several Vietnamese were arrested in the Buddhist struggle against the Ky/Thieu government. Stories leaked out, messages were smuggled out, and occasionally someone was released. One, jailed for participation in an anti-government peace demonstration was released, became an officer in the Saigon army and now has been imprisoned again. He described life in jail:

> "I was put in prison with all kinds of people -- a former Under-Secretary of the Ministry of Interior, an army officer who had studied mathematics at the University of Illinois, an attache at the Vietnamese Embassy in France, a 75-year-old farmer, a cyclo driver and a woman with PhD's from three different countries. In the women's section, babies were born in prison, breast-fed and were two years old by the time I left. How quickly time flies!"

In the March 24, 1969 issue of The Nation, he wrote:

> "In those jails most cells were about 5 feet by 9 feet, built in French colonial times to house two or three natives each. The modern Vietnamese mandarins, after receiving their 'mandate of heaven' from the imperialists, somehow managed to cram ten or twelve 'independent' Vietnamese into each cell. They picked up money from the Americans on a per capita basis to feed us, and occasionally American 'Advisor mandarins' would show up with their Vietnamese 'counterparts,' to discuss, measure, calculate new rooms. They looked proud and solemn. Yet conditions became steadily more crowded, even with the building of new, modern-style cell blocks with interior partitions and carefully painted walls (always in red and black--perhaps a form of psychological torture?). How scientific these Americans!"

In the same article he described the torture that went on in the prison:

> "A few 'important' prisoners were interrogated directly by CIA officials, often in English and without interpreters. Such prisoners were rarely tortured. By contract, 'ordinary' or 'low-class' prisoners were questioned with the aid of electric coils, kicks to the head, chest and stomach, the head forced under water. Girls had bottles forced up the vaginas, men were struck with gun butts, squeezed with pliers, beaten with hammers, nailed through the legs and arms."

One of the largest groups of prisoners are farm people who have been picked up in military sweeps or by the Phoenix operation. In 1967, a member of the International Voluntary Services (IVS) program in Viet Nam described what had happened to a hamlet of refugees and "VC suspects" that had been brought into the destrict headquarters where he had been assigned to help take care of refugees:

> "I have seen blind-folded men, their hands tied behind them, thrown out of helicopters -- the helicopter was only 3 feet off the ground, but the blind-folded men couldn't know that. They would collapse in shivering heaps when they hit the ground, and often would have to be dragged away from the helicopter so it could land. I have watched while these same men, still blind-folded and tied, were made to run down a steep hill, at the bottom of which were three rows of concertina barbed wire. The first row would hit them across the knees and they would plunge head first into the second and third rows of wire. They lie there until they are dragged out and sent skidding down another hill, at the bottom of which there is not barbed wire--their only defense is to collapse into a shivering heap on the ground--but that is sure to earn a few kicks and orders, given in English, to stand up if they want the kicks to stop. The VC suspects are then relieved of all their money (it goes into the mess fund or pays for prostitutes), they are asked their names and put in jail without food or water for the first 24 hours (or more). An interrogation session begins with a beating. The prisoner is not tied or blind-folded but he must in no way defend himself, a question is asked and before he can answer he is kicked in the chest or stomach or hit in the face--again a question and again no answer is allowed. By noontime the Americans involved are soaking their sore fists and having the interpreter do the work. In the end it turns out that some were VC, others weren't. 'Xin Loi* about that.' In the meantime the wives and children of the men being interrogated are doing unpaid labor--some of the children were kept in the jail--there was no food or shelter provided for anyone, and for the first day all 350 people were confined within a barbed wire circle in the middle of a field."

---

*Xin Loi means Sorry.

The IVS refugee worker described the American soldiers who brought the refugees in and sometimes tortured them:

> "The GIs I know and work with are not professional interrogators or intelligence men. They are average people with average feelings. They believe it is necessary to be here and probably necessary to burn an occasional village, but they don't like it and the things they see and do, worry them. In order to ease their consciences, their officers constantly point to 'sacrifices' that other Americans are making to help the Vietnamese, and then point to the 'ingratitude' on the part of the Vietnamese people. I have been informed by well meaning men that the Vietnamese do not love their families, do not like children, enjoy pain and suffering, don't care if they live or die and love killing. With some shade of this attitude in their minds and the 'glorious' image of the young American sacrificing his time and money to help such heathens, the conscience can be quieted and justified."

The rural people are caught in the middle. One resident of a hamlet in Quang Tin province said that many of his neighbors had been arrested and either killed or taken away to prison. This man said that the Phoenix operation, an American financed program to destroy the communist infrastructure, was responsible for most of the arrests. He explained it this way:

> "In my hamlet, the Phoenix men come at night and rap on our doors. They are dressed in the black pajamas of the Liberation soldiers and tell the people they are with the Liberation army. But they are really the secret police. If the people welcome them with joy, these policemen kill them or take them off as Viet Cong. But if they are Viet Cong soldiers and we say anything good about the Saigon government, we are taken off as rice bearers or soldiers for the Front."

"A day in a Vietnamese prison is a thousand years," a high school student at Can Tho's Phan Thanh Gian High School said of the Can Tho prison. He had been imprisoned in that jail for several months for suspected peace activities in his high school. The prison was built for 500 prisoners. In 1968 there were 1700 prisoners and a few pigs. Its odor was the heavy, sweet smell of human bodies that sticks to the visitor's clothes for hours after he walks out of the prison.

The failure to separate inmates by age, health, or type of crime is one of the most depressing aspects of Vietnamese prisons.

Giao, a 12-year-old shoeshine boy, was arrested for sleeping on a movie theater rooftop in 1968. Unable to pay the policeman the normal fifty cent bribe, he was put in the Chanh Hung jail for three months. There were about 100 prisoners in the same room--other shoeshine boys, dope addicts, beggars, thieves, feeble-minded, and two convicted murderers. Obvious symptoms of T.B. and other diseases were evident among many of the prisoners. "What we need is someone to keep the prisoners from spitting on the facilities," an American prison advisor told the director of one relief organization while discussing what a voluntary agency could do to help the prisons.

The treatment of prisoners became an especially important political issue in the Spring of 1970. Several students who had been active in anti-government demonstrations were jailed. On April 20, a trial was held at the Military Field Court for 17 of the arrested students. The students arrived in obviously bad physical condition. Some were being carried by others, they were emaciated and their faces haggard.

Immediately following the April 20 trial, ten students were released. The reason for their release is not clear--one of the released students said it was "because they had no reason to arrest us in the first place," and one of Saigon's better-known lawyers who had followed the case closely said the government wanted these students to serve as an example to other students who might be thinking of going onto the streets to demonstrate. The ten released students put themselves on display at an anatomy laboratory in the College of Agriculture.

Do Huu But was in semi-shock and fed dextrose intravenously. His fingernails were blackened. "Pins and slivers of wood," a student said. He appeared to be deaf. "Soapy water was put into his ears and then his ears were beaten," another student said.

Mrs. Cao Thi Que Huong claimed she had been beaten by police clubs. Her knees were swollen three times their normal size and black-and-blue welts covered her tiny arms.

She said she had been undressed in front of several policemen who drank whiskey and laughed and cheered at the more spectacular forms of torture.

(Photo by Don Luce)

Unable to pay a policeman a 50-cent bribe, the shoeshine boys often end up in prison.

(Photo by Don Luce)

Gaio, a 12-year old shoeshine boy, was arrested for sleeping on a movie theater roof-top. He is shown here on the day of his arrest with the prison wall in the background.

"When they wanted me to sign papers, they tortured my husband while I was forced to watch. When they wanted him to sign papers, he was brought in while I was being tortured," Mrs. Que Huong said.

Luu Hoang Thao, Deputy Chairman of the Van Hanh Student Association, described what happened to him after he was arrested on March 13:

> "For the first three days, the police beat me continuously. They didn't ask me any questions or to sign anything. They just beat my knee caps and neck with their billy clubs. Then they beat me with chair legs. When a chair leg broke, they took another one. I was beaten until I was unconscious. When I regained consciousness, they beat me again. Finally, after three days, they asked me to sign a paper that they had already written.

> "They read the paper, but they would not let me see it," Thao said. "I wouldn't sign it, so they beat me some more."

> "They put pins under my fingernails. They attached electrodes to my ears, my tongue and my penis. They forced soapy water into my mouth, tramping on my stomach when it became bloated with the water. Then they hung me from the ceiling and extinguished lighted cigarettes in my nipples and penis."

Leo Dorsey, a volunteer social worker with the Unitarian Universalist Service Committee in Viet Nam, went to the U.S. Embassy to request an interview with Ambassador Ellsworth Bunker for a small group of volunteers concerned by the use of U.S. equipment to support the Saigon government's repression (the tear gas was made by Federal Laboratories, Inc. in Saltsburg, Pennsylvania; the jeeps that carried off arrested peace demonstrators have the symbol of American aid, the handclasp, conspicuously displayed on their doors; the police and prisons receive more than twice as much U.S. economic aid as the Vietnamese education system). Ambassador Bunker's office said the ambassador could not meet with the group and referred them to Ambassador Berger. Ambassador Berger's office said Ambassador Berger could not meet them and said the appropriate office was Youth Affairs. Youth Affairs said they could not comment on this and that the place to go was Public Safety. The Public Safety Director would not see them, but an appointment was finally made (more than a month later) to see Mr. Randolph Berkeley, Chief of the Corrections and Detention Division of the American economic aid effort who would not discuss the torture because "that takes place in the Police Interrogation Centers and the PIC are not under the Corrections and Detention Branch's area."

"Generally speaking we have found the Vietnamese very light in their punishment," Mr. Berkeley said. "Prisoners in Viet Nam are very docile. Once they're arrested you could lead them around with a string. The prisons are controlled by very few personnel--only 1000 for the 32,000 prisoners in the Correction Centers. This is a ratio of one to 32. We have to have many more guards per thousand prisoners in the U.S."

In response to a question about assistance to the prisons by voluntary agencies, Mr. Berkeley said that "the head of the prisons does not want to get involved with social welfare organizations. He is afraid that they will cause him more trouble than they will help."

Mr. Berkeley outlined the major objectives of his division. First of all, he said, they had to keep the prisons secure. "In 1967, the NLF entered three prisons, freed 2000 prisoners, gave them weapons and put 'em to work." Secondly, the U.S. was assisting in a program to expand the prisons to take care of an increasing number of prisoners and to prevent over-crowding. "In the early days, we had a problem of knowing who was in the prisons and how many prisoners we had. In 1967, for example, there was a problem of people suffocating in the Can Tho prison because of overcrowding."

"There are three different prison systems here for civilians," Berkeley said. "First, there are the Correction Centers with 4 national centers (including Con Son) and 37 provincial centers. Then there are 64 screening and detention centers. Finally, there are the Provincial Interrogation Centers."

"Can you tell us more about the Provincial Interrogation Centers?" Leo Dorsey asked.

"No, I can't. They aren't under our jurisdiction."

"Does the United States have advisors in them?"

"Yes."

"Who provides these advisors?"

"I can't tell you that."

"Are they military or civilian?"

"Look, you boys better keep out of this question. You might get yourselves hurt."

Mr. Berkeley insisted that Con Son was a model prison and that the U.S. was proud of its advisory efforts there. He stressed the freedom given the inmates and the vocational training program there.

"It is the largest prison in the Free World," he said. "Ten thousand prisoners and it's growing all the time."

In 1970, a Vietnamese who will be called Hoa here to protect his identity, was released from the Tiger Cages of Con Son prison. Hoa wanted to get word to as many people as possible about what was happening in Con Son prison.

At that time a delegation of ten U.S. congressmen were visiting Viet Nam. Three of them, Donald Clancy of Cincinnati, Ohio, Robert Mollohan of Fairmont, West Virginia, and Albert Watson of Columbia, South Carolina, were scheduled to visit a South Vietnamese prison. "That way we can put pressure on the bastards in the North to let us in their POW camps," one of the three said.

Hoa met one Congressman not scheduled to visit a prison, Augustus Hawkins of Los Angeles. Hawkins, concerned about what was going on at Con Son, invited other congressmen to his hotel room to hear what Hoa had to say. Clancy and Mollohan came.

"I am a student at the University of Saigon studying to be a teacher," Hoa told the Congressmen. "In 1968, I opposed the new draft law which said that male students who had not entered the university by the time they were 19, could not receive an exemption from military service. Instead they would be drafted. This law discriminates against the poor. The rich can afford the best high schools and necessary tutors to pass the difficult exams. The poor often must leave school for a year or two or maintain part-time jobs. At a time when hopes for peace were rising, Thieu was recruiting more soldiers and increasing the intensity of the war."

"What happened to you when you were arrested?" Congressman Hawkins asked.

"I was taken to the Central Police Headquarters where I was beaten by the police. They asked me to sign a paper saying I was a communist. I refused. They beat me some more and asked me to sign their papers. I told them that I was not a communist, but that I was a student studying to be a teacher who was opposed to war.

"They tied by hands behind my back and suspended me from the ceiling by a rope. That was especially painful. Then they beat me some more."

"When were you taken to Con Son prison?" Congressman Clancy asked.

"I was taken to Con Son Island on April 15, 1969, in Navy boat #403. We were all chained to iron bars. If there had been a storm and a lot of water taken into the boat, we would have drowned. It is against international law to lock prisoners in this way when transporting them on the high seas. At that time we were reminded of the 18th century when black slaves were transported from Africa to your country. We were so afraid."

"What happened when you got to the island," Congressman Clancy interrupted, obviously irritated at Hoa's long descriptions.

"When we got to the island we were met by 300 order guards. These are prisoners who are there for criminal acts like robbery, murder and rape. By agreeing to guard the other prisoners, they are given special privileges. We were lined up and marched off. Each of us had to keep our heads bent to the ground. There was one old man from Bien Hoa who could not keep up. He was too weak. The orderlies beat and kicked and cursed him. They hit him on the head with a cane. 'Slowness means being whipped. Do you hear, boy?' They would say this and hit him again. This old man suffered more than anyone else that day."

"I've got to get to bed," Representative Clancy interrupted. "We've got a long day tomorrow."

Then in an aside to Representative Mollohan, he said, "I don't see much difference between young people here and in the States. They all exaggerate."

"After one day," Hoa continued, "I was sent to the Tiger Cages where I was shackled with four other prisoners in a tiny room three meters (10 feet) long and 1 1/2 meters (5 feet) wide. For 14 months I lived in that cage.

"We did not get enough to eat. Water was so scarce that we drank each others' urine. We collected it all and then divided it evenly. But, because no one had enough water to drink, it was very bitter. We had to lie there all day. We could not rise up nor could we talk to each other."

"Why did they let you out?" Congressman Mollohan asked. He, too, was bothered by the length of the answers and it was nearly 11:00 p.m.

33

"I was let out because the students here have demonstrated for the release of prisoners unjustly sentenced. Now I am working to help make known the plight of my friends who are still in the Tiger Cages. Only when their plight is known will they get enough water to drink and food to eat. They have done no crime. Those in the Tiger Cages are political prisoners who dared to speak for peace."

"I have some advice for you, young man," Representative Mollohan said to the 27-year-old Hoa. "You have a political system here. Work through that system. You've got elections coming up. Work for the man you want to see elected. Don't go around causing trouble. You're only going to get thrown back into the Tiger Cages and you won't do anyone any good there."

"I've been travelling around Viet Nam a lot in the last few days," Congressman Mollohan replied. "And I've seen some good things. Things aren't perfect. But things are improving."

The Congressman started to get up, but was held in place by the intensity of the young man before him:

"This is what the French told my people. Each year things were getting better. It is what you Americans told us in the reign of General Khanh. And it is what you were telling us while you helped Ky and Thieu destroy the Buddhists in 1966. Now you tell me that everything is getting better while my little brother rots in the prison at Con Son, while hundreds of my friends are forced to drink bitter urine in the Tiger Cages. And I should vote because things are so much better..." he stopped then and smiled sadly. "I'm sorry. I'm very sorry. I should not talk like this to a guest in our country. But please do go to Con Son. Please try to find out what is going on there."

The next day the three Congressmen--Clancy, Mollohan and Watson--backed out. Because the story of the young man was too preposterous to believe? because they did not want to believe it?? or were they suddenly just too busy with other things??? But Representative Hawkins had listened carefully throughout the evening and was deeply moved. He would go. At breakfast the next morning, Congressional Aide Harkins, who had sat in on the meeting with Hoa, learned of the decision of the original three not to go. He angrily told the others about the conversation the night before. Congressman William Anderson, former commander of the nuclear submarine, the Nautilus, listened to Tom and said quietly: I will go.

The logistics of setting up the trip gave us little time to invite a Vietnamese delegation to go on the trip. Most important, the Congressman wanted Deputy Ho Ngoc Cu to accompany them. Deputy Cu was Chairman of the Vietnamese National Assembly Committee of Interior. Unfortunately Deputy Cu could not go.

"I would like to go very much," he told us. "But I must be present when the city election results for councilmen are verified. Your trip is very important. We have heard many stories about the Tiger Cages of Con Son. I believe they exist, but when I went to the prison I was told they did not exist. A year ago I asked for improvements in the prison system. But to tell you the truth, little has been done. Conditions are still very bad. In Vietnam, we have a very close family system. When you do an injustice to one man, you alienate his whole family. The conditions in our prisons are making communists, not only in the prisons, but also outside.

"When you treat one many unjustly here," Deputy Cu continued, "you make 50 enemies. The whole family will work against you. We must have a revolutionary reform in our prisons. The inmates must be given enough food to eat, enough water to drink. Correction and vocational training must be emphasized rather than punishment."

"What kind of advisors do you think the U.S. should send to Viet Nam?" Tom Harkin asked.

"When you send Americans here, please send those who have love in their hearts for other people," Mr. Cu replied.

The night before the trip to Con Son, Hoa prepared detailed descriptions of the prison: a map of the island showing the locations of the different camps; a map showing the location of the Tiger Cages within Camp Four; another map showing how to get to the "Cattle Pens"; descriptions of the identification badges worn by prisoners, yellow with orange stripes for those held without trial, green and red for military political prisoners (who had carried on anti-Thieu activities or encouraged desertion while in the army), green and yellow for military criminal prisoners; and yellow for civilian criminal prisoners. The orderlies, Hoa said, would be made up of the last two categories and wear yellow armbands or have a number "1" on their badge.

Hoa gave the names of six specific prisoners to ask to see: four students including Hoa's younger brother, the editor of a French-language newspaper, and one of Hoa's former cellmates. (He gave us detailed descriptions of each of these men in case the prison administration tried to fool the congressmen).

Finally, Hoa provided a list of questions to ask:

>   --How often have you had vegetables? Meat?

>   --Did you get a special meal today (because of our coming)?

>   --Did you get special clothes today?

>   --Is medicine available for the sick?

>   --Have you ever received a letter or package?

>   --Did you have any money when you arrived? What happened to it?

>   --What happened to Ho Van Chin (Hoa claims he was killed on May 10, 1970)?

>   --Have you been beaten?

>   --When did you last have a bath?

>   --Are the orderlies Chin Rong and Chin Khuong still here (two orderlies with reputation of
>   being especially vicious)?

"You will never find the Tiger Cages," Hoa insisted. "Many people have tried to find them before and failed. There is only one way. You must go through the tiny door at the end of the path where the vegetables are grown. But they will not let you find that. They pile wood up in front of that door so, even if you get close, you cannot get in. They will stall and feed you and give you long briefings. But you won't see the Tiger Cages...unless you take me. I know them very well. You must take me."

But the Congressmen could not take Hoa. The personal danger was too great for him even if he could get on the airplane. Also, the prison authorities would have been immediately suspicious if a former inmate of the Tiger Cages had been with the congressmen.

"I believe you want to help my people," Hoa told the congressmen as they left. "I believe you want to see an end to this injustice. Perhaps I will be arrested again; perhaps I will be shot in a dark alley. But this is not important in comparison to the work of ending the horror in the jails. You worry about me because you have seen me laugh and talk. I am a person to you. But I have seen ten thousand other people who have been and are still being tortured. Each one of these ten thousand is a person to me. That is why it is important. My younger brother is there; my friends who lived 14 months in the cages with me are there; Ho Hieu and Nguyen Truong Con, Chu Quyen, Chu Ba and Ho Hung Van are there. As a man, I cannot rest until these men are able to live free as I do now."

(personal note: I do not know where Hoa is today. I have made inquiry after inquiry--both through his friends in the Vietnamese student movement and through the NLF. No one knows what has happened to him. Perhaps he is back in the Tiger Cages or perhaps he did "disappear" in a dark alley. But I like to think he is doing what he wanted most to do: teaching in a village school somewhere.   Don Luce)

APPENDIX A

THE TIGER CAGES OF CON SON

by Don Luce

(Editorial Note: This description of Con Son was written on the eve that the group visited that prison island.)

Con Son Island -- "The tiger cages existed during the time of the French. It was the most inhuman kind of treatment you can imagine. Prisoners were shackled to iron bars in tiny cages and deprived of physical necessities and human dignity. But these cages no longer exist."

This was the official position of prison authorities in Vietnam before a Congressional Committee. The committee included Congressman Augustus Hawkins of the Los Angeles Watts area, Congressman William Anderson, former commander of the Nautilus submarine, Thomas Harkin, a congressional aide, and myself. A group from the U.S. Public Safety Office accompanied us.

Con Son prison is located in the South China Sea approximately 140 miles southeast of Saigon. It is Vietnam's largest civilian prison, having 9,916 prisoners as of June 1970 according to the U.S. Public Safety Director of Vietnam. Its seven camps have a total capacity of 9,750 inmates (about 2,000 trustees now have housing outside the seven camps). The prison was established in 1862 by the French. Sometimes called "Devil's Island," mention of the name Con Son brings fear to most Vietnamese. Although Ho Chi Minh was never imprisoned there. it was also called "University of Ho Chi Minh" because so many of its "graduates" changed from a strong anti-communist position when they entered to joining the Viet Minh on their release.

No, Con Son is not like Alcatraz or a "Devil's Island," claimed Frank E. Walton, Director of the U.S. Public Safety program in Vietnam at the beginning of the trip, commenting: "This (place) is more like a Boy Scout Recreational Camp."

But there had been other stories. After considerable pressure from the Vietnamese student movement, five students were released from Con Son where they claimed they had been held under terrible conditions in the same tiger cages that the French had used. They wrote in a report to the Vietnamese National Assembly:

"Living under these conditions lacking food, clothing and shelter, the prisoners had to endure confusion and serious disease. Food was inadequate, beatings were regular, feet were shackled day and night. Most of our fellow prisoners in the cages were paralysed, not to mention the number suffering from chronic dysentery, tuberculosis due to long-term physical exhaustion; stomach disorders from the beating by trustees, from eating sand and pebbles in the rice, from being forced to eat too fast, gangrenous feet from a lack of vitamins, and endless other diseases.... Medicine was dispensed as the person in charge of medical problems was inspired to do so. Here, every time we wanted to ask for medicine we had to wait until we were in agony and then we generally only received a few aspirin tablets. Any medicine more valuable than this was all hoarded by the orderlies and their accomplices in the administration and was taken away and sold."

Was their story true? The two Congressmen went to Con Son to investigate. Earlier three Congressmen had backed out after two of them had heard detailed descriptions of the conditions in the tiger cages by a former inmate. It all seemed too preposterous. For a time it appeared that none of the Congressmen would go -- but due to the hard work of aide Thomas Harkin and Anderson the trip was made.

As the airplane approached the beautiful island of Con Son we read the prepared briefing:

"The Con Son Island National Correction Center, located in the South China Sea approximately 140 miles southeast of Saigon, is Vietnam's largest correctional institution. Established by the French in 1892 as a penal colony, it has long held a reputation of being a "Devil's Island." This reputation still prevails, in spite of an enlightened and modern administration of the facility."

We were preplexed. Former inmates had related tales of horror, yet, the American advisors spoke in glowing terms. Other investigation teams had found nothing. No Westerners had seen the cages since the time of the French (or at least none would confirm their existence.) "There are no tiger cages. Only a thing of the past," everyone had been told who visited the island by the officials. Yet they had left unconvinced because the prisoners on the island had told them secretly "you must see the tiger cages."

36

At 9:58, after a twenty-minute drive from the airport, we began discussions with the Chief Warden, Col. Nguyen Van Ve. We talked about the plane ride and the beautiful island. "Con Son means Mountain Island," Col. Ve explained cordially. At 10:10 a prison guard brought us cafe filtre -- the kind of coffee that drips slowly into your cup drop by drop while you wait. The conversation went on slowly.

At 10:23 Thomas Harkin abruptly changed the discussion about the weather and mountain. "Would it be possible to talk to some individual prisoners," he asked.

"Why yes. of course," Colonel Ve said in his impeccable English, smiling. He could arrange that.

"We have a list of names of people we would like to see," Harkin said. "These are some people we have learned are here and we would like to see them."

A cloud passed over the face of Colonel Ve as he reached over to receive the list of six names.

"You must have permission from the Ministry of Interior if you want to see specific individuals," he said after reading the names. "You can't just come here and see anyone you want. This is a prison."

"We have come to investigate all aspects of American aid here and we would like to get as accurate a picture as we can," Congressman Hawkins explained. "Perhaps you could telegram the Ministry of Interior to ask permission."

At this point, Frank Walton, the top U.S. prison advisor commented angrily: "We thought this trip was above-board. If you had wanted to see specific individuals, you should have informed us first. This is sneaky and unethical."

Colonel Ve then reverted to Vietnamese,using the U.S. Public Safety Division's interpreter to translate: "I'll send a message to the Ministry of Interior, but they cannot respond before eleven o'clock when you are scheduled to leave for Saigon."

"Oh, we can stay a few extra minutes," Congressman Hawkins said. "Perhaps we can go to see the prison wards now. Do you have a map of the island showing the location of the camps?"

"I'm afraid we don't," Colonel Ve said. When questioned further, Colonel Ve explained in Vietnamese that the camps were so small and the island so big that the camp locations would seem insignificant on a map of the island. But before this was translated, Mr. Walton interrupted and explained that security reasons did not allow them to make such a map. "The VC might get hold of it and come and release all the prisoners."

It was now 10:40 and, according to our schedule we were supposed to leave to catch the plane. At that point Colonel Ve went to his desk to give final instructions on sending the telegram to Saigon to get permission to see the specific six prisoners. "Whether they (Saigon) answer or not is not important," he told his aide in Vietnamese who was questioning the wording (at this point, they still did not know that I spoke Vietnamese).

"Why don't we go over to the curio shop?" Mr. Walton suggested. "They have some really nice things like the swagger stick that Col. Ve has. It's just across the road. It would be nice for you to have some souvenirs to take back to the U.S."

"I'd like to see the prison camps," Congressman Hawkins replied. "We can pick up the souvenirs when we finish the tour of the prison sites."

The group then loaded itself into three jeeps and went to camp number 2. The prisoners were lined up, faces tightened into stiff, frightened masks.

At the infirmary, medical care to the prisoners was explained.

"We have a doctor who treats each patient separately. Medical care here meets modern standards."

The sick prisoners were asked a few questions by the congressmen:

"Do you get enough to eat?"

"Yes, plenty. Rice, dried fish, and vegetables," one answered.

"Do you receive medicine?"

"Yes, we get medicine every day."

As the questioning went on, I wandered over and talked to a man alone. He told me:

"I am a political prisoner from the time of Diem. I have no idea when I'll be released. It is so bad here. Do you see the man who is so sick? He has received no medicine until today when they put the bottle with water up (a dextrose bottle was being used to feed him intravenously).   That was for you to see. No medicine. No vegetables..."

37

At this point a gaurd came up and he continued:

"Everything is quite good here. It is not like the mainland but we have plenty to eat and the people here are kind."

As I walked away, he pleaded with his frightened eyes.

That was the first time that the prison administration realized I spoke Vietnamese. From then on they made a desperate attempt to keep me from speaking to any prisoner alone.

In response to a question about whether the inmates had a chance to play sports, Randolph Berkeley, Chief of the Corrections and Detention Division of the U.S. Public Safety advisory program said:

"Colonel Ve even plays soccer with the prisoners. He is so well liked!"

"I play soccer with them on Sunday afternoon," Col. Ve said picking up the cue. "And sometimes they beat me -- but I don't even punish them," Colonel Ve laughed pleasantly at his joke.

Congressman Hawkins suggested that we go on to Camp 4. We all got into the jeeps and were taken to Camp 5. I was asked to interpret by Thomas Harkin. This time a guard was standing by:

>   "Where are you from?"
>   "Ben Tre."
>   "When were you arrested?"
>   "Ten years ago."
>   "Why were you arrested?"
>   "I am a political prisoner."
>   "But what was the specific reason?"
>   "The provincial authorities arrested me."
>   "You were arrested because you are a traitor," the guard prompted.
>   "I was arrested because I am a traitor," the prisoner parroted.

In another case, a prisoner said he did not know why he was arrested.

"You had a grenade in your hand and you were planning to kill people. Isn't that true?" Colonel Ve shouted authoritatively.

"I had a grenade in my hand and was going to kill people," the prisoner said.

It was the same, situation after situation. Yes, the food was delicious - when the guards were around. No, we have almost no food, they said, when the guards were not around. Yes, we get letters from home -- when the guards stood by and listened. No, we cannot receive or send letters - when the guards were not listening.

After Camp 5, Representative Hawkins made his request once again to see Camp 4. It was there we had been told the infamous tiger cages were. As we entered the compound of Camp 4, it was as it had been described and as we had put together clues from various people. Two wells on one end with Chinese imperial type decorative walls in front of the wells. Some beautiful flowers which one of the Representatives photographed. But what we could not see at first was the small alley which was supposed to be between the wall of one of the prison buildings and the outer wall. Thomas Harkin saw it first - a narrow path between the two walls with some vegetables growing along the side for the trustees. He passed the word on.

"It is good to see that you have an agricultural project here, Colonel," Representative Hawkins observed. "What are these plants?"

"These are called Vietnamese spinach," Colonel Ve replied. "We encourage the prisoners to plant things after they become trustees."

"Not really enough to feed many people though," the Congressman observed as he worked his way to the far end of the alley. "By the way, where does this little door lead to?"

We started to shake the door and rap on it. It was a tiny door, hardly large enough for one person to enter.

"Oh, that goes to another camp," Col Ve replied. "We can enter through the other side."

We looked at each other, remembering the words of one person who knew the location of the tiger cages: "There is only one way. You must go through the tiny door at the end of the path where the vegetables are grown."

"I'm tired," Representative Hawkins said. "Can't you send someone around to open the door? We can wait here."

"The Congressman is tired. Can you send someone around to open the door?" Thomas Harkin repeated the request.

"This door is always locked. You can't get in," the Colonel said.

Then miraculously someone came to the gate from the other side to see what was the matter. He opened the door and we slipped through. There before us were the tiger cages. We climbed to the top and looked down onto the prisoners huddled in the cages, three or four in each cage.

The tiger cages are small stone compartments. Inside each cage is a wooden bucket for sanitary purposes which is emptied once a day. The cages are not quite five feet across and about nine feet long. There were three prisoners in each one. To see them we climbed up a stairway and looked down on the prisoners through an opening at the top which is crossed with iron bars. There were 60 or 70 cages in the building.

We looked down onto the prisoners huddled in the cages.

(left to right: Don Luce, Augustus Hawkins, and William Anderson.)

(PHOTO BY TOM HARKIN)

Model showing the Tiger Cages.
The buckets hold caustic lime.

"Donnez-moi d'eau," one prisoner said in French.

"I am sorry I cannot speak French," I answered in Vietnamese, not trusting my poor high school French. "But I speak Vietnamese. This is a Congressional team from the United States who have come to look into prison conditions in Vietnam."

"We are thirsty. We are hungry. We have been beaten," one said and the chant was picked up.

"I am here because I spoke for peace. That is what all Vietnamese want. We only ask for peace," said another.

As we walked down the aisle above them, the prisoners pointed to sores on their bodies. One man showed us his hand. Three fingers were missing.

"They cut off my fingers when they arrested me," he said. Then he turned his head and showed us a big scar on the back of his head.

None of the men could stand up. Until a few days ago, they said they had been shackled to a bar that went across one end of the cage. The bars had just been removed (although the bars were still left in the cages) but the slots to put them back in were still there.

"We will be shackled again in a few days," one said as he crawled around the cage using his hands to move himself.

One of the prisoners pointed to the scars on his useless legs and said, "We were shackled here for months. We are hungry, thirsty and sick. Please give us some water."

"I am a Buddhist monk and I spoke for peace in 1966. I am here for no reason except wanting peace. I have been beaten. I have been shackled. But I still speak out for peace."

(PHOTO BY TOM HARKIN)

Buddhist Monk in Tiger Cage

40

Above each cell was a wooden bucket of lime.

"What is this for?" we asked Col. Ve.
"The lime is to white wash the walls," the colonel said.
"No! No!" the prisoners shouted. "It is thrown on us when we ask for food."

The floors of many of the cages were covered with lime.

"When it is thrown on us, we cough and spit blood. Many of us now have the disease of the lungs (T.B.) and it is so difficult to breathe when the lime is thrown on us."

"There are other tiger cages. You must see them too," we were told. "There are cages with women. We hear them screaming and they are near. Right over there."

We climbed down the stairs and went to the adjacent building. Here was another double row of cages identical to the ones in the men's side. Every cage was filled with five women. The women ranged in age from fifteen years old to one old, blind lady, who must have been nearly 70.

"Please give us some water. Please give us some food," they pleaded.

"We have been here seven months and have had a vegetable three times in these seven months."
"We are beaten and sick and yet we don't have any medicines."

Many of the women were obviously very sick. Some had T.B.; some had eye diseases; most had skin diseases. Those who were in the worst condition lay on the floor of the tiny cages while others fanned them with odd bits of cloth.

"How old are you?" I asked one beautiful young girl.
"Eighteen."
"Are you a student?"
"No, I am a laborer. I worked in a factory."
"Why were you arrested?"
"I was in a peace demonstration."
"Are you a Communist?"

At this, the young girl laughed at what seemed to her an irrelevant question.

"No, I am not a Communist. I am not concerned about politics. I am concerned about peace."
"Will you salute the flag?" the guard who was standing beside me demanded
"No! No! I will not salute your flag which represents all the things you have done to me," she answered definantly.
"Then you are a Communist and should be killed," the guard retorted in equally bitter tones.

Many of the girls were young students from Saigon's most prestigious schools like Gia Long, Madame Curie, etc..

"We can only wash every two or three days and then we have almost no water," they said. "During our menstration period it is very hard because we cannot wash ourselves properly. That is not sanitary."

There are about 500 people in the tiger cages. They are hungry, thirsty and show obvious signs of having been beaten many times.

As we left the tiger cages, we were confronted once again by Frank Walton, head of the U.S. Public Safety Division.

"You have no right to interfere with Vietnamese affairs," he told us. "You have cone here trying to stir up trouble. You are guests of Colonel Ve here. You aren't supposed to go poking your nose into doors that aren't your business."

"But this is our business," Congressman Hawkins explained. "The United States gives considerable aid to these prisons. We want to be sure our aid is used in a humane way. Several American boys are being held prisoner in North Vietnam. I hope they are not being treated the same way as are the prisoners I have just seen being treated here."

"You are judging the whole prison of 10,000 inmates on how four or five hundred are being treated. This prison is equal to the standards of many of the prisons in our own country," Walton said.

"These are very bad people," Colonel Ve told us. "They will not salute the flag. They will not even salute the American flag."

We then went back to the headquarters of the prison island where Colonel Ve apologised for not having lunch for us (it was now past one o'clock) and because he had still not received word from the Ministry of Interior about the Congressman's request to see six specific prisoners.

"I am sorry I have no luncheon prepared," he said. "I thought you were leaving at eleven this morning."

'That's alright, Colonel," Representative Hawkins said. "But I would like to go to that curio shop. I'd like to get me one of those swagger sticks."

But the curio shop was closed.

The conditions we saw at Con Son were very different from the "fact sheet" which had been passed out on our departure from Saigon that had stated:

"The inmates are kept busy with work projects and vocational tasks such as woodcutting, tile making, woodmaking, animal husbandry, chicken and duck production and sewing. Inmates also attend classes in literacy training, and all grades of formal education. Rice, papayas, coconuts and vegetables grown on the prison farm and fish caught by the prisoners supplement the diet...In the opinion of Correction Advisors with lengthy U.S. penology experience. Con Son is not a "Devil's Island," but on the contrary is a correctional institution worthy of higher ratings than some prisons in the United States."

A better description is the last words we heard as we left the tiger cages:

    "Please give us some water."

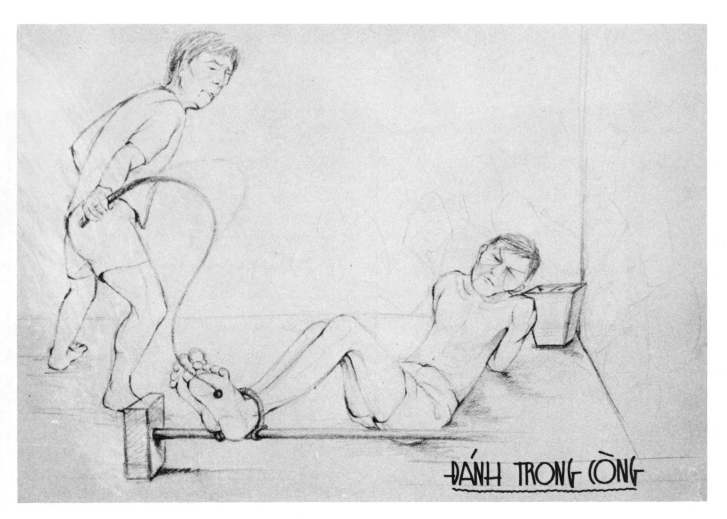

"Beating in Cell"
Drawing by former Tiger Cages inmate

NEW TIGER CAGES BUILT BY UNITED STATES

Following the international outcry against the tiger cages, the Saigon Government announced they were going to do away with them. But two months later, they ordered the political prisoners who were not paralyzed from previous shackling to build new ones as a "self-help" project. The prisoners refused, were put into shackles and on January 7, 1971 the United States Dept. of Navy gave a $400,000 contract to Raymond, Morrison, Knudson-Brown, Root and Jones to build 384 new "isolation cells" to replace the Tiger Cages

These new "isolation cells," wrote Colgate S. Prentice of the U.S. Dept. of State are six feet by eight feet -- two square feet <u>smaller</u> than the former Tiger Cages. The new "Tiger Cages" are worse in every way than the former ones, Vietnamese who have been released from the island claim.

When the U.S. began construction on the new cages, the Vietnamese weekly, <u>Con Ong</u> (The Bee), printed an editorial cartoon. President Nixon was shown unloading the new Tiger Cages and asking if the Vietnamese weren't happy to get this new aid. Yes, said the Vietnamese sarcastically, looking up. It was needed more than schools, hospitals, churches, pagodas or clothing. That issue was confiscated a few hours after it went onto the streets.

CONTRACT FOR NEW TIGER CAGES
DEPARTMENT OF THE NAVY

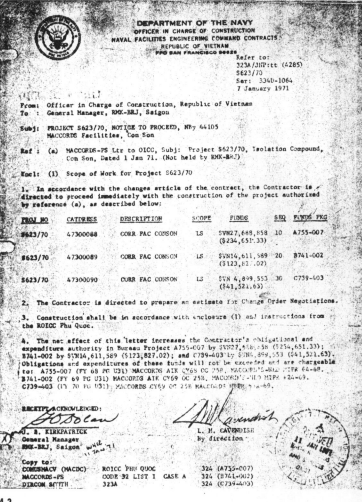

43

APPENDIX C

Report from American Friends Service Committee Representative, Saigon, June 18, 1972

INTERVIEW WITH A PUBLIC SAFETY ADVISOR

Several days ago, I entered the office of a CORDS Special Assistant for Public Safety, in order to ask for some information to write an article: the present size of the Vietnamese National Police Force, its growth rate over the last few years, the amount of American aid that has gone into it. After consulting with a senior Public Safety Advisor, the man assured me that he was not trying to be uncooperative, but that his office never gave out information to the press and that I would have to go through a military information officer.

He explained that the Public Safety Directorate is particularly sensitive about reporters "using" even the simplest of facts in a sensational way and not doing enough research to understand the full story. "Nothing in public safety", he told me, "is simple."

"To show you how damaging irresponsible reporting can be," he said, "there were two stories written about Con Son prison which cost the American taxpayers $400,000."

I asked if he was referring to the famous "tiger cage" story, but he said "I'm not going to tell you any more." In spite of himself, though, he began to warm up to the subject and went right on.

"The people who wrote those articles for Life and Time didn't know what they were talking about, and as a result, $400,000 and hundreds of hours of advising time were wasted to fix something that was never wrong in the first place."

"You mean to say there was nothing wrong with conditions on Con Son?"

"No," he replied, and then indicated that the infamous prison island compared favorably with some American prisons.

I said I had seen the pictures of the tiger cages in Life Magazine and they looked pretty bad to me.

"You think a picture can't lie?" he said. "I'll show you two ways those pictures gave a distorted impression. First: the article said the tiger cages were under ground, but in fact all cells on Con Son are above ground. Whoever took the pictures had to climb up one and a half stories to look down on the cells. The article didn't explain that, did it?"

Having made his first point easily, he moved into the second one with relish. "Second," he continued, "remember the picture looking down into the cage? You could see through the bars and there was a man's face looking up from underneath - the face was very clear. Now, anybody who knows anything about photography can tell you that the bars and the face couldn't both be in focus! Now, the article pointed out some white fuzzy stuff on the bars and claimed it was lime that they throw down on the prisoners, when in fact it was only the fuzziness of the out-of-focus bars!"

And then, to give the final touch to his argument, he added: "Besides, the lime they use for prisoner control out on Con Son is this color", pointing to a manila folder on his desk, "not white".

He never did tell me the size of the Vietnamese National Police force.

Diane Jones

APPENDIX D

3000 WOMEN, CHILDREN AND OLD PEOPLE RECENTLY DEPORTED TO THE PRISONS OF CON SON

(Editorial Note: This document was prepared by the Committee to Reform the Prison System in South Vietnam in August 1972)

The Con Son affair became known thanks to a letter sent to a priest by an administrative employee working on this prison island. The foreign press,1/ has published this letter. As for the Saigon press, only the review Doi Dien (Face to Face) has dared to publish it.

The deportees on Con Son were passed off by the Saigon authorities as refugees from communism. The fact is that the Central Vietnam administration, after the Quang Tri offensive, whipped up an organized campaign of repression and arrest against the population, which was then deported to Con Son. The general pattern of the arrests was as follows: the inhabitants were summoned to "settle certain matters"; they were then arrested and forced on ships bound for the island.

A special boat, which left Central Vietnam on May 7th and arrived at Con Son on May 11th transported 1,500 deportees. Of these, only 142 had had any sort of trial. Nearly all of them are inhabitants of the region Hue (Phu Cam, Phu Soc, Can Hai). The majority of them are old-folk, women and children. The number of very young children (infants and under 9 years) is about 50 to 70. This figure will increase as there are a number of pregnant women among the deportees. Some of them gave birth as soon as they arrived on the island. At present numerous of pregnant women are afflicted with nervous crises and symptoms of madness because of their separation from their husbands and worries about their children. Moreover, the conditions of life are extremely wretched. Medical supplies are inadequate. The children are the first victims because there is a shortage of milk.

It must be noted that these people are unable to comprehend why they have been forcibly deported as "refugees". One can cite the dramatic case of a woman of 73. Her husband is dead. All of her six sons are in the Saigon Army; three of them have died in combat. She lived in Van Xa and had gone to see one of her surviving sons who was stationed in Saigon. The son wanted her to remain near him, but she wanted to go back to Central Vietnam to live near the tombs of her ancestors. There, she was arrested and accused of having "contact" with "the other side". She was transferred to Con Son as a "refugee from communism."

An appeal, together with the relevant documents, has been addressed to Monsigneur Nguyen Van Binh. The letter begs the Archbishop of Saigon, as a man of conscience and as a religious leader, to intervene and bring help to these people, deported as "refugees from communism" to Con Son.

When the affair was revealed, a delegation undertook to visit the island. This delegation was composed solely of military almoners and two Americans: a Protestant clergyman-advisor and a Catholic priest, a Director of Catholic American aid.

The composition of the delegation was as follows:

1) Colonel Phan Phat Huong, priest, deputy Director of the general army Catholic alms-services.
2) Lieutenant-Colonel Dinh Ngoc Que, priest, chief almoner for the special zone of the capital.
3) The almoner for the division of Gia Dinh.
4) McVeigh, priest, director of American aid.
5) Colonel Miller, clergyman, general advisor to the military alms-houses in Vietnam and his 12 escorts.

The gifts taken by the delegation included:

1) 4000 pairs of trousers, offered by Mme Nguyen Van Thieu, wife of the President
2) 150,000 piastres [300 US dollars] offered by Father McVeigh, director of Catholic American aid.
3) 50,000 piastres [100 US dollars] for the children, offered by Monseigneur Nguyen Kim Diem, archbishop of Hue.

1/
   Le Monde, 14 July 1972

The delegation flew to Con Son on July 21st. On arrival, having been unable to meet the deportees, the delegation simply handed over the gifts through the intermediary of a number of representatives. After this visit, public opinion began to ask a number of questions.

The affair is still in the air. It is certain that numerous citizens have been deported to Con Son (and even to Phu Quoc) in recent months without anybody having been told about it. Certain Saigon newspapers have recently revealed that the U.S. and South Vietnamese counter-intelligence departments from March 29th (the beginning of the Quang Tri offensive) until July 18th, "accused" and then deported about 3000 people from Central Vietnam, of whom 862 were arrested in Hue. Among them, there are, it appears, 2 venerable Buddhists; the rest are inhabitants of Da Nang and Binh Dinh.

" Detainees suspected of being Viet Cong, are transported to the rear area for further interrogation by authorities. . . " (Caption and Photo by the United States government) Throughout the Viet Nam war, thousands of farm people have been arrested, tagged and sent off for interrogation.

APPENDIX E

THE LAWS OF VIET NAM

(Editorial Note: The laws in Section II are all in effect and form the basis for most of the arrests and certain laws, such as Article 19 of Decree-Law number 004/66, provide the "justification" for not holding court trials.   The basic freedoms "guaranteed" by the Constitution (Section I) are no longer respected: martial law is in effect and Constitutional freedoms suspended by the Decree-Laws.)

I. Selected Articles from the Constitution of the Saigon Government

Article 1

1. Viet Nam is an independent, unified, and territorially indivisible Republic.
2. Sovereignty resides in the whole people.

Article 2

1. The State recognizes and guarantees the basic rights of every citizen.
2. The State advocates equality of all citizens without discrimination as to sex, religion, race or political party. Minority compatriots will receive special support so that they can keep up with the pace of progress of the population as a whole.
3. Every citizen has the duty to serve the interests of the Nation and the People.

Article 4

1. The Republic of Viet Nam opposes Communism in any form.
2. Every activity designed to publicize or carry out communism is prohibited.

Article 5

1. The Republic of Viet Nam shall comply with those provisions of international law which are not contrary to its national sovereignty and the principle of equality between nations.
2. The Republic of Viet Nam is determined to oppose all forms of aggression and strives to contribute to the building of international peace and security.

Article 6

1. The State respects human dignity.
2. The law protects the freedom, life, property, and honor of every citizen.

Article 7

1. The State respects and protects the security of each individual and the right of every citizen to plead his case before a Court of Law.
2. No one can be arrested or detained without a legal order issued by an agency with judicial powers conferred upon it by law, except in case of *flagrante delicto*.
3. The accused and his next of kin must be informed of the accusation against him with-in the time limit prescribed by law. Detentions must be controlled by an agency of the judiciary.
4. No citizen can be tortured, threatened or forced to confess.
   A confession obtained by torture, threat or coercion will not be considered as valid evidence.
5. A defendant is entitled to a speedy and public trial.
6. A defendant has the right to a defense lawyer for counsel in every phase of the interrogation, including the preliminary investigation.
7. Any person accused of a minor offense who does not have a record of more than three months imprisonment for an intentional crime may be released pending trial, provided that he or she is employed and has a fixed residence. Women pregnant more than three months accused of minor offenses who are employed and

have a fixed residence can be released pending trial.

8. Accused persons will be considered innocent until sentence recognizing their guilt is handed down. In event of doubt, the court will rule in favor of the accused.
9. If unjustly detained, a person has the right to demand, in accordance with the provisions of the law, compensation for damages from the State after he has been pronounced innocent.
10. No one can be detained for indebtedness.

Article 8

1. The private life, home, and correspondence of the citizen must be respected.
2. No one has the right to enter, search the residence and confiscate the property of a citizen unless in possession of a court order, or when this is necessary to the protection of public security and order within the limits of law.
3. Privacy of correspondence is protected by law. Any restriction imposed on this right must be determined by law.

Article 9

1. The State respects and guarantees the freedom of religious belief and the freedom of every citizen to preach and practice religion as long as it does not infringe upon the national interest and is not harmful to public safety and order or contrary to good morals.
2. No religion is recognized as the State religion. The State is impartial in the development of various religions.

Article 12

1. The State respects freedom of thought, speech, press, and publishing as long as it does not harm personal honor, national security, or good morals.
2. Censorship is not accepted except for motion pictures and the theater.
3. Press regulations will be prescribed by law.

Article 13

1. Every citizen has the right to meet and form associations within the framework of the law.
2. Every citizen has the right to vote, run for office, and participate in public affairs on an equal basis and in accordance with conditions and procedures prescribed by law.
3. The State respects the political rights of all citizens, including the right to petition freely and engage in overt, non-violent, and legal opposition.

Article 14

Every citizen enjoys freedom to choose his place of residence and freedom of movement including the right to go and return from abroad except when these freedoms are restricted by law for reasons of public health, security, and defense.

Article 16

Freedom to join labor unions and to strike is respected within the framework and procedures of the law.

Article 29

Any restriction upon the basic right of the citizens must be prescribed by law, and the time and place within which such a restriction is in force must be clearly specified. In any event the essence of all the basic rights of the citizens cannot be violated.

II. Decree-Laws Used to Justify Political Arrests

A. Decree-Law 93/SL/CT of February 1964

Article 1   By this Decree are outlawed private persons, parties, leagues, associations that commit acts of any form which are, directly or indirectly, aimed at practicing Communism or Pro-Communist Neutralism.

Article 2   Shall be considered as Pro-Communist Neutralist a person who commits acts of propaganda for and incitement of Neutralism; these acts are assimilated to acts of jeopardizing public security. (Note of the translator: The act of jeopardizing public security is punished by Article 91 para 3 of the South Viet Nam Revised Code of Criminal Laws with a maximum penalty of 5 years imprisonment.)

Saigon, February 1, 1964

Signed: Major General
NGUYEN KHANH

B. Decree-Law 215/SL/CT of August 1964

Article 1   There is hereby proclaimed a State of Emergency throughout the territory of Viet Nam, as of this date until further order.

Article 2   Any law or regulation which shall be deemed necessary not to be applied may be declared temporarily suspended.

> Saigon, August 7, 1964
>
> Signed: Lt. General
> NGUYEN KHANH

C. Decree-Law 004/65 of May 1965

Article 1   The following acts will be within scope of an subject to the punishments provided for in the Decree-Law 093-SL/CT dated February 1, 1964:

a. All acts directly or indirectly aimed at disseminating policies, slogans or directives of the Communists or of individuals and organizations controlled or influenced by the Communists.
b. All campaigns that in effect weaken the anti-communist spirit of the nation and cause prejudice to the struggle of the Armed Forces and the people, including plots and acts serving the Communist cause that are camouflaged as peace or neutralist movements and similar acts.
c. Dissemination, circulation, distribution, offer to the public, sale, display in public or storage for the same purposes, of publications, pictures and communications through other media that have the above effects.

> PHAN KHAC SUU

D. Ordinance No. 01/UBLDQG of June 1965

Article 1   There is hereby, proclaimed a State of War throughout the territory of Viet Nam.

Article 2   During the State of War, the Central Executive Committee is delegated the power to take appropriate measures for safeguarding the territory of the country and the public security and order.

> June 24, 1965
>
> Chairman of the National
> Leadership Committee
>
> Major General NGUYEN VAN THIEU

E. Decree-Law 004/65 of July 1965

Article 1   In order to safeguard the public security and order to the utmost, particularly serious punishments are applied to the offenses listed in this Decree-Law during the state of war.

Article 10   Are sentenced to solitary confinement with hard labor those youths:

- Who use fraudulent manners or tricks so as to avoid presenting themselves when they reach the age to fulfill their military obligations.
- Who make themselves physically disabled or ask other persons to cause their physical disability so as to avoid the fulfillment of their military obligations, either temporarily or permanently.

The principle offender and his accomplices are sentenced to the same penalties.

Article 11   It will be considered as a failure to report for induction and the offender will be sentenced to as follows:

- Solitary confinement with hard labor: those who are duly notified to report for induction but fail to report to the designated place within 20 clear days including the day mentioned in the order; those who enlist or re-enlist but fail to report to the designated place within a period of 20 clear days, including the day mentioned in the travel orders.
- Three years of imprisonment: A citizen who knows that his particular draft registration number is printed in a public notice for induction or re-induction but fails to present himself to the military authority of the place where he resides for the regularization of his status within a period of 15 days, commencing on the dates mentioned in the public notice.

Article 12 Is sentenced to solitary confinement with hard labor any member of the Commission of Mobilization Census, the committee of draft exemption or draft adjournment, or the Medical Examination Committee, who, upon being requested to give opinions or to conduct any examination,

- promises to assist or incites young men or servicemen to avoid their military obligations.
- falsifies papers concerning military obligations so as to assist or incite young men or servicemen to apply for exemption from or delay of military service.

Article 13 Are sentenced to a penalty of a term from five years of solitary confinement with hard labor for a term of years all servicemen of the regular, Regional, and Popular Forces, members of public forces, and personnel of various public services (including regular, contractual and journey personnel) who, within a time-limit of 15 days, without rightful cause, refuse to carry out an order of transfer or appointment, or an order for an official mission issued by the rightful authorities in command.

If the breach is committed by a band or with intent to impede the functioning of the public service, the maximum penalty will be applied.

Article 14 Any person who joins a Communist organization or collaborates with the Communists, to bear arms against the country, shall be punished by sentence of death and a total or partial confiscation of his property. In case the offender is a serviceman, this violation also brings about his military degradation.

Article 15 Is sentenced to death any person:

- who rebels or incites other armed people to rebel, or recruits soldiers and furnishes them with weapons and ammunitions without order or authorization from the government.
- who, without authority, voluntarily takes command of a platoon, a warship, a wing of airplanes, a sea port or a city.

Article 16 Is sentenced to solitary confinement with hard labor for life any person who excites the mob by organizing meetings or demonstrations with the purpose to disturb the security of the state.

Article 17 Is sentenced to hard labor for a term of years any person:

- who directly or indirectly disseminates any policy, slogan, or directive of the communists, or of an individual or a league influenced or controlled by the Communists.
- who commits any act in order to undermine the anti-communist spirit of the country, or to cause harmful effect to the struggle of the people and the Armed Forces.
- who plots to act under disguised signification of peace or neutralism in accordance with communist doctrine.
- who popularizes, circulates, distributes, brings to public attention, sells, exhibits at public places, or conceals with those purposes, any printed materials, pictures, or other media, so as to attain the purposes mentioned in the above three paragraphs.

Article 24 Throughout the State of War the military field courts will have jurisdiction over the offences set out in this Decree-Law in accordance with procedures prescribed in Decree-Law No. 11/62 of May 21, 1962 establishing the Military Field Courts.

Article 25 Once culpability has been established, the court is not authorized to give consideration to extenuating circumstances for the accused.

Saigon, July 19, 1965

Signed: Major General
NGUYEN VAN THIEU

F. Decree-Law 004/66 of February 1966

Decree-Law No. 004/66 dated 15 February 1966, complementing Decree-Law No. 4/65 dated July 19, 1965 relative to the punishment of speculation illegal transfer of funds, smuggling, bribery, influence peddling, violations of public security, embezzlement of public funds, rebellion, hooliganism, communist sympathizers and neutralists.

Article 11 Three years imprisonment: Any citizen who knows he is called or recalled to military service whether under a collective draft or not and fails to report to the military authorities at his place of residence within 15 full days after the date prescribed in the public announcement.

Article 19 Those persons considered dangerous to the national defense and public security may be interned in a prison or designated area, or banished from designated areas for a maximum period of two years, which is renewable; the internment and banishment shall be ordered by Arrete of the Prime Minister issued upon the recommendation of the Minister of Interior.

The same Arrete shall also order the disposal of any properties used in activities dangerous to national defense and public security.

An internee who escapes or attempts to escape from the area of internment or forced residence shall be liable to Reclusion.

Article 22   Those persons who gather in assemblage of two or more and attack, resist or obstruct the public force personnel in their duties shall be punished with death.

The killing of offenders in self defense shall be excused.

Saigon, February 15, 1966

Major General NGUYEN VAN THIEU

G. Decree-Law 015/66 of April 1966

Article 1   As long as the State of War lasts as proclaimed over the territory of the Republic of Viet Nam and from the dated of promulgation of the present Decree-Law, all military personnel guilty of desertion, all abettors and accomplices of deserters shall be sentenced in accordance with the special punitive measures as set forth below:

Article 2   Punishments for desertion shall be as follows:

- Death: if the deserter abandoned his unit to join the enemy or the rebels.
- Hard labor for life: if he deserted in the presence of the enemy or rebels.
- Hard labor for a specified duration:if he deserted while his unit was not engaged in operation or has received orders to engage in operations.
- 5 years of solitary confinement with hard labor in case he deserted while his unit was not engaged in operations or if he deserted in such circumstances as are specified in the Code of Military Justice and the punishments prescribed therein are lighter than that provided herein.

Article 3   When serving their sentence, convicted deserters shall not be kept in jails but shall be sent directly to the field to serve in special Coolies of the Battlefield Units.

Article 4   Convicted deserters shall automatically receive the supplementary punishment of military degradation, be deprived of their rights to pay and allowances, and in the case of death shall be deprived of the right to be recognized as having died for the country, and of the right to any subsidy of any kind for the widow. In case of wound or infirmity, they shall not be entitled to any subsidy or compensation-allowance.

Article 5   While serving their sentence, if they escape:

- the first time, the sentence previously adjudged shall be doubled;
- the second time, they shall be sentenced to death.

Article 6   In case they already have been convicted for desertion and sentenced in application of punitive measures specified in the present decree law, and have thereafter been rehabilitated, if they desert again, the sentence shall increase by one degree.

Article 7

a. Any person [1] who by whatever means, whether effective or not, incites or promotes desertion shall if he is military be sentenced to the same sentence as adjudged to the deserter and shall serve his sentence the same way as does the deserter; if he is a civilian, he shall be sentenced to 5 years of solitary confinement with hard labor.
b. Any person convicted of having intentionally given assistance of any kind, harbored a deserter or concealed a deserter shall, if he is military, be sentenced to the same punishment as adjudged to the deserter; he shall serve his sentence the same way as does the deserter. If he is a civilian he shall be sentenced to 5 years of solitary confinement with hard labor.
c. As for commercial industrial firms and liberal profession practitioners, the court may either order the closing of the firms or the cessation of practice, or the temporary suspension thereof.

---

[1]

(Editorial Note: For example, a Buddhist monk opposed to killing.)

Article 9   In case their guilt is recognized bu the Courts, no mitigating circumstances may be considered in favor of the accused, except in case they have voluntarily turned themselves in.

Saigon, April 21, 1966
Signed: Major General
NGUYEN VAN THIEU

H. Decree-Law 1763 ND/AN of September 1966

Decree-Law No. 1763 ND/AN of September 24, 1966 delegating to the Minister of National Security the authority to order deterrent measures against persons regarded as dangerous to the National Defense or Public Security.

Article 1   There is hereby delegated to the Minister of National Security the power to pronounce by order the following deterrent measures, of administrative internment in a prison or compulsory residence in a designated area or banishment from certain local areas, for a maximum period of 2 years, which may be extended at the expiration.

The Minister of National Security will be responsible for deciding the disposition of objects, money or other property involved in activities dangerous to the National Defense or Public Security, as prescribed in Article 19 of Decree-Law 004/66 dated February 15, 1966.

Saigon, September 24, 1966

Vice Air Marshall
NGUYEN CAO KY

I. Decree-Law No. 004/TT/SLU of July 15, 1972,

Article 1   In the war or martial law situation those caught wandering during the hours of curfew without a written authorization, or a valid excuse such as birth-giving, an unexpected illness requiring emergency treatment, etc., will be subject to a prison sentence ranging from 6 days to 2 months, or fined from 1,000 to 10,000 piastres.

Article 2   In the war or martial law situation those presently detained or placed under house arrest by government decision who attempt, or are planning an attempt, to escape, will be severely punished.

Article 3   In the war or martial law situation all forms of labor strikes and disputes, even those that have gone through a process of mediation, and even if its only purpose is to provide mutual support to resolve a labor conflict, will be strictly forbidden.

Article 9   In the war or martial law situation those who organize demonstrations or gatherings considered detrimental to national security will be severely punished; those who attend [such meetings] will be jailed from 1 to 6 months.

Signed: NGUYEN VAN THIEU

THE PRESENT SITUATION OF CHI HOA PRISON

South Vietnam's Chi Hoa Prison now contains nearly 10,000 prisoners of all types, from political detainees, ie. those people who are regarded as opposed to the present regime of South Vietnam, to offenders of "ordinary crimes" such as forgery, theft, drug addiction... For the present time, political offenders, regarded as "an element danger-ous and harmful to the national security," are sent to Chi Hoa Prison at a rate of about 100 a month. As for people accused of "ordinary crimes," nearly 1,000 of them are put in Chi Hoa every month. Meanwhile, rare are released prisoners, none of these are political detainees.

Under extremely unfavorable conditions caused by tight repressive measures of the Director of Chi Hoa, we have tried to do our utmost to find out all the facts revealing the real nature of the so-called "Saigon Re-Education Center" by which the government of Nguyen Van Thieu has boasted of having improved the penitentiary system of South Vietnam.

I. Administrative Policies

One of the general principles applied by the government of Nguyen Van Thieu to the administration of prisoners at Chi Hoa as well as almost all the prisons in South Vietnam is "use of prisoners to rule their own inmates." In all compounds (or sections), the direction of Chi Hoa has assigned prisoners to the "Order and Security" Services. These prisoners are allowed to beat other inmates as they please and usually are "acknowledged" scoundrels, rapists or gang rapists...(Here are some examples:)

- Tran Van Loc, Chief of the "Order" Service, Compound FG, concurrently Head of Room #1F2. Imprisoned at Chi Hoa on charge of willful aggravated assault after extortion of all jewels and money, committed against a woman. Sentenced to 5 years' imprisonment.

- Nguyen Van Chi, Chief of the "Order" Service, Compound ED, concurrently Head of Room #OD3. Imprisoned at Chi Hoa on charge of robbery under aggravating circumstances and gang rape. Sentenced to 5 years' imprisonment.

Especially in the rooms of offenders of "ordinary crimes," hooligans hold all the posts of the Room's Representative Committee. They always resort to violence, brutal beatings to cow inmates:

- Le Viet Dung, nicknamed Dung "Mexico", Head of Criminal Room #3G2, once the terror of Saigon people with his murders, lootings, rapes..., was arrested with his gang after a "night affair." At Chi Hoa, Dung "Mexico" and his men of the gang were all assigned to posts of Room's Representative Committee. Every week, 3 or 4 inmates become victims of their brutal beatings.

In political detainees' rooms, the policy applied is always one of repression by dividing inmates and infiltrating undercover agents of the Secret Police to report to the Center's Security Bureau every strike of the inmates as well as their demands for better food or progressive people.

- At Room #2G4, an undercover agent of the government, named Nguyen Van Hoang, was assigned to the post of Head of Room with the aim of preventing all the inmates' struggles and denouncing to the direction those of real patriotism.

II. Activities At Chi Hoa Prison

None of the so-called "re-education" programs are organized for political detainees or offenders of "ordinary crimes" at Chi Hoa Prison. Prisoners are only accorded religious services; yet, these services are usually not free but forced to attend. Of strongest influence at Chi Hoa Prison are Protestant and Catholic religions.

(Here are some cases of forced attendance at religious services:)

- Nguyen Hoang Quan, Prison Registration No. 3991GC, now at Room #3F3, Compound Fg. Ordered to attend a "weekly talk" by Protestant ministers on Wednesday, Sept.6, 1972, Quan refused to, was beaten brutally by the Room's "Representative Committee," then brought to the Center's Security Bureau to be "cuffed" at both feet. Four weeks later, he was transferred to another Compound on charge of slandering religions and resist-ing the Representative Committee.

- Ngo Dong Thai, Prison Registration No. 1296GCGD, Room #2B2, Compound BC. Forced to attend a Mass organized every week at the Center on Tuesday, Sept. 12, 1972; the man in charge of this religious service is the Catholic priest named Tran Van Thong. Thai was obliged to go to this service for fear of being beaten by the Room's Representative Committee, but did not attend it to the end. He returned to his room and later was summoned by the said priest and beaten right in the chapel, then brought to the Center's Security Bureau for more punishment. (Father Tran Van Thong is a terror for prisoners at Chi Hoa because he is even more brutal than the wardens. Well-known for his cruelty and cunning, he was nicknamed the "Devil Priest" by prisoners.)

Daily life at Chi Hoa Prison is simply tragic. A room here is only about 6 meters by 8 meters (about 19 feet by 26 feet), yet, contains more than 100 persons and includes only 0,4 meter by 0,8 meter (or about 1 foot 3 inches by 2 feet 7 inches). So, it is really overcrowded and unhealthy. This usually causes abscesses and various diseases among prisoners. At present, Room #1G2 of Compound FG contains 181 prisonsers; many of these have to find a place to sleep in the corridor.

In addition, the food provided is insufficient and particularly bad. Their food intake for a meal is just five (5) piasters. This includes rice and other food. Each prisoner of ordinary crimes is supposedly offered 50 grams of fish and 50 grams of vegetables, but actually he has never been provided with the whole of his portion. His rice is always half-cooked, mixed with ashes and dirt. For other food, he gets ill-smelling ready-boiled fish and some wilted vegetables which have turned yellow. Each room of more than one hundred prisoners is given 36 kilograms of ready-cooked rice and about 30 grams of vegetables and fish a day.

As for political detainees, thanks to hard struggles at the cost of their own life, they are given each about 120 grams of vegetables and 120 grams of fish a day. But their portion of rice is by no means better than that of prisoners of ordinary crimes. And they also receive ill-smelling spoilt fish and yellow wilted vegetables which are only supplied them after 3 or 4 days in stock.

In general, one may say that prisoners at Chi Hoa Prison are not provided with sufficient food. As a result of this, they either get sick easily or become skinny and weak.

III. The Imprisonment Of Children Under 16

Chi Hoa Prison is not aimed at training or re-educating arrested children. These children are just a natural consequence of the corruption of the Nguyen Van Thieu regime, and an inevitable outcome of the society full of injustices of South Vietnam. All this is merely a plot to dominate the people of Vietnam through the lackey administration of Nguyen Van Thieu by poisoning and corrupting the progressive spirit of the youths of South Vietnam. That is the reason why our juvenile delinquents are far from being reformed after their release from Chi Hoa Prison. In fact, they do commit more crimes.

In addition, we have to mention a greater number of youngsters, who are unjustly arrested but soon learn from their young fellow inmates at Chi Hoa such bad practices as stealing and gathering together to battle against each other...

- Nguyen Van Vinh, aged 12, ran away from home a long time ago. Arrested early this year (1972), charged with robbery in the street, awaiting trail. Prison Registration No. 4019GC, now detained in Room #0B2, Compound BC. After nearly one year at Chi Hoa Prison, Vinh has learned smoking marijuana with his fellows with the money stolen from other inmates.

- Tran Van Than, aged 14, arrested in April, 1972, accused of being an accomplice in a gang rape, and of robbery. After almost half a year of imprisonment, Than has gathered a number of his Room's fellow inmates together to steal the personal effects of new prisoners then sell them. Every youngster in his gang know how to inject drugs to himself. Than is now detained at Room #0C4, Compound BC. Prison Registration No. 6215GC. This is the 3rd time he has been arrested after 2 evasions from Thu Duc Reformatory (in Gia Dinh Province.)

IV. Murders At Chi Hoa Prison

Prisoners of ordinary crimes now detained at Chi Hoa usually gather together in different gangs to fight against each other whenever there is a dispute between their gangs. Murders occur very often right in Chi Hoa Prison. Policemen are sent there by the government to investigate and report whenever there is a prisoner killed. Weapons often used by killers in Chi Hoa Prison are knives, bottles ... or sometimes even heavy pickaxes provided them by wardens.

- Tran Van Le, Chief of the Labor Service #0E4 and head of a gang of "acknowledged" hooligans, killed a prisoner member of Lam Seo's (the scarred Lam) gang on Sept. 4, 1972. Using a heavy hammer, Le broke in Lam Seo's room when this was already closed; then with the same hammer, he struck one of the members of Lam Seo's gang heavy blows on the head and killed him right on the spot. He also stabbed at a number of other inmates. Some of these latter had to be taken to outside hospitals for medical treatment. Wardens of this Compound FG are almost all accomplices with the gang of Tran Van Le; so they did nothing to stop Le when he broke in Lam Seo's room. This murder is due to the trade of smuggled drugs in prison.

- Nguyen Ngoc Van, aged 24, inmate of Room # 2BC, Compound BC, murdered a member of this room's Representative Committee out of rage. Van had sharpened a chopstick, and taking advantage of the dark when everyone went to bed, pricked it into the ear of Tu who was sleeping soundly. Tu was bleeding to death a little more than one hour later. Doctors at Chi Hoa were powerless in this case. This murder occurred in July, 1972.

V. Corruption At Chi Hoa Prison

Corruption is widespread at Chi Hoa Prison. There is corruption from the director down to head of every room (ward). We got to know that Lieutenant Colonel Do Tan Duc, Director of Chi Hoa, is a confidential man of Prime Minister Tran Thien Khiem. And as such, Colonel Duc has no fear of being transferred and exploits prisoners as he pleases.

1. Corruption of the Director

Every inmate who wants to return home for a visit has to pay a sum to the Director. This sum varies, depending on the duration of the visit. Usually, if this is for 24 hours, one has to pay VN$ 30,000.1/ For about 36 hours the sum is VN$ 40,0C0.

- Mr. Qui, assistant director of the Nha Be Depot of the Shell Company. Arrested with his followers on charge of stealing gas. Right after their arrival at Chi Hoa, Qui and his followers paid half a million piasters to the Director of Chi Hoa to be allowed to return home for a visit and to stay at Compound AB, the reserved quarters for the rich and foreigners.

Besides, the Director of Chi Hoa also gets money from rich prisoners who want to be transferred away from their room or compound. These people pay at least VN$ 30,000 to be tranferred to Compound AB, VN$ 40,000 to be transferred to Compound AH.

In addition, there are other forms of corruption such as stealing from the food rations of prisoners, taking bribes from religious persons who want to carry on their propaganda (in the prison) such as Protestants...

2. Corruption of the Wardens

Wardens at Chi Hoa are people of the same stock as the police of the government. These wardens have also gathered together with hooligan prisoners for the trade of objects prohibited by the rule of the Prison, such as sharp knives, heroin, marijuana, radio, newspapers... Usually, wardens also get money from those inmates who want to be heads of their wards. The price of this post varies, as follows:

- VN$ 40,000 for the post of Head of the Labor Service,
- VN$ 30,000 for the post of Head of Room (or ward) of Prisoners of ordinary crimes,
- VN$ 60,000 for the post of the Head of Room of Drug Addicts, and
- VN$ 80,000 for the post of Head of Room of Foreigners.

For a post in the "Order" Service of the prison, one has to give wardens at least VN$ 5,000. To be in the "Security" Service, the minimum price is VN$ 10,000. Prisoners who do not want to do the labor service when ordered to, have to pay at least VN$ 2,000. Besides, there are rather important briberies for gamblings and trade of drugs in prison...

3. Corruption of the Head of Room (or Ward)

As presented above, heads of Room are arrested "acknowledged" scoundrels who pay for their post in prison to get advantages for themselves by exploiting other inmates or enjoy those same privileges given them by the direction itself. After all, this is essentially exploitation of others.

- Tran Van Nam, Prison Registration No. 1295GCCD, Head of Room of Chinese #3G1, Compound FG. Bought the post of Head of his room with a sum of VN$ 60,000. Every month, sent his family at least VN$ 30,000. This money comes from his exploitation of inmates. Each new inmate in the room has to pay VN$ 1,000. After every visit of his family, he has to pay an additional sum of 300 piasters. That is to say nothing of his obligatory contribution to the Room's fund for various imaginary necessities such as lamps, soap... imposed on him by the head of his room.

- Le Ky, aged 32, Secretary of Compound FG (a title corresponding to that of Chief of the "Order" Service). Sent over VN$ 40,000 to his family every month. This money comes from his arrangements with heads of room to send new prisoners to these person's rooms. These heads of room share the money with him since each new prisoner in their room has to pay a minimum of VN$ 500. He also has the right to transfer inmates from one room to another after proposing to the Chief of Compound. (His proposal is of course easily accepted).

- Nguyen Ngoc Lam, aged 26, Head of Room of Drug Addicts. Paid VN$ 60,000 for his post. Sent his family at least over VN$ 50,000 a month. This comes from his collusion with wardens in trading heroin, opium... as well as the same manuevers of any other heads of rooms.

These authentic facts we have just mentioned show that corruption at Chi Hoa Prison is as well organized and widespread as in any other institution of the present government of South Vietnam. Corruption at Chi Hoa Prison is indeed outrageous - acts of exploitation of inmates. None of their victims dare to resist these barbaric practices for fear of being ill-treated at the risk of their own life.

1/
    The official exchange rate at the time this was written was VN$ 450 equals US$ 1.

VI. Drugs and the Game of "So De" 2/

A. Drugs:

It is a real inconsistency on the part of the Nguyen Van Thieu government when it, by order, prohibits the use of drugs, arrests drug addicts...and at the same time, at Chi Hoa Prison, offenders of this crime, who number easily 1,000 person, are allowed to use drugs all the same, provided they offer enough money, i.e. much more money than they need to have drugs outside. As we have mentioned in Part V, it is the wardens who provide drugs to make profits. For an example, the price of drugs at Chi Hoa Prison is given here:

- 1 cc. of opium for intravenous injection costs 150 piastres in prison instead of only 40 or 50 piastres outside.
- A small capsule of heroin costs at least 2,000 piastres and is now very difficult to obtain. This same amount costs 600 to 800 piastres outside.

Most of these addicts now in prison prefer drugs for injection for their relatively cheap price and do not consider their more dangerous effects. The government does not offer these inmates any treatment and merely confines them in ill-smelling, dirty dark cells (solitary confinement). Most of the murders at Chi Hoa come from these cells of drug addicts. The lack of drugs for injection or smoking causes disputes and stealing among these addicts leading to their killings. The lack of drugs also causes diseases and finally death. The deaths from this cause are numerous at Chi Hoa.

Case Histories of the Trade in Drugs at Chi Hoa

- Warden Nguyen Van Lanh, a stairway guard at Compound FG, carries on himself a lot of drugs whenever he is on duty. In collusion with such heads of rooms of drug addicts as Lam, Trinh, and Thanh, he has sold these drugs to inmates at very high prices mentioned above, three times as much as what he pays outside.

- Warden Phung Huy Vuong, of Compound ED, sells various kinds of hypodermic syringe (eye-dropper) for drug injection at the price of 2,000 piastres each and pipes for opium-smoking at nearly 5,000 piastres each.

The government of Nguyen Van Thieu has called upon the people to crush this vice and threatened to imprison gamblers; yet, ridiculously the game is held right in the prison, by the wardens themselves and sometimes in collusion with outside organizations. Whenever an inmate wins at this game of chance, the warden who organizes the game will come to give the prize (money) to the winner.

- Warden Tran Van Muoi, nicknamed Muoi Le (Muoi the squint-eyed), aged about 50, sits in the corridor of Compound FG, to receive the bets from inmates in the early morning of every Tuesday (the winning numbers of the "Reconstruction" National Lottery are drawn in the afternoon of the same day). He pays the winners, if there are any, in the following afternoon.

- Nguyen Dang An, warden of Compound BC, is another man who receives the bets from inmates of Chi Hoa.

The Game of "So De", just another form of gambling, has been spreading widely and openly. From this sort of gambling, each warden can get about VN$ 50,000 a month.

All the facts we could gather from Chi Hoa Prison prove that as long as the Nguyen Van Thieu regime and the American intervention in South Vietnam persist, the penitentiary system cannot be improved, and to cover the corruption of the present regime of South Vietnam. That is why the "Committee for the Improvement of the Penitentiary System" of a number of progressive intellectuals in South Vietnam has on many occasion called upon the Nguyen Van Thieu government to carry out a general reform of prisons in South Vietnam. But their demands for reform have been all turned down.

2/

   "So De", a game of chance, consists of betting on 2,3 or 4 numbers on certain rows of numbers of the prized tickets which come out every week at the drawing of the National Lottery. People who play this game inform the numbers of their choice and give their stake to a "head of game" or the representative of this latter. For this, they get a receipt which is "good for the game" but legally of no value. If they are lucky, they can get 80,800 or 8,000 times as much as their stake (depending on whether they bet on 2,3 or 4 numbers).

   This game of chance (originally known as "the game of 36 animals") is closely attached to the government-controlled National Lottery; yet, it is privately organized (probably by the Chinese).

   It is widespread in every circle of the population of South Vietnam, including government workers. And there is no doubt that many chiefs of provinces and chiefs of police are in collusion with those at the head of the organization of the game for fabulous bribes.

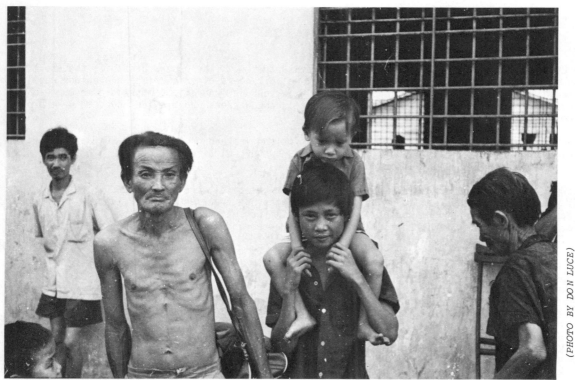

(PHOTO BY DON LUCE)

The prisoners are not sorted by age or even by whether ill or healthy.
All of these prisoners were in one cell.

(PHOTO BY DON LUCE)

Whole families are imprisoned. . . the Chanh Hung prison mess hall.

APPENDIX G

ARREST OF MEMBERS OF THE COMMITTEE FOR THE REFORM OF THE PRISON SYSTEM OF SOUTH VIETNAM

(Editorial Note: This is part of the testimony sent on August 20, 1972 to the International Assembly of Christians, 122 West Franklin Avenue, Minneapolis, Minnesota by the Committee for Reform of the Prison System of South Vietnam.)

At this time the Committee for Reform of the Prison System of South Vietnam has had to cease all activity. Some of its members are under arrest; others have been obliged to go underground. The few members who are still in liberty, such as Professor Nguyen Van Trung, president of the Committee, live in a state of constant anxiety knowing that they are under close surveillance and that they could be arrested at any time.

Recently Father Chan Tin sent to the President of the Senate a letter concerning the arrest of a certain number of the members of the Committee at the time of a visit to the Lodging center for Former Prisoners.

A. Letter To The President Of The Senate Of Saigon By The Reverend Father Chan Tin

Mister President,

We have been greatly shocked by the repression and arbitrary threats of the last few days which the administration has leveled against a social action recognized here and abroad as in the public interest. It is the matter of aid to former prisoners released into liberty in view of their return to normal life.

After much effort, with the warm support of all levels of the population, with the participation of a large number of notables, of religious leaders, of deputies and senators in office - one of whom is a senator of your party who presides over the judicial council - with the support of several international organizations, we have been able to set up a lodging-center for the purpose of receiving, helping, and guiding former prisoners released into liberty, without discrimination as to the reasons (political or common law) for their imprisonment. This lodging-center is presently located at 9, on national highway No. 1, commune of Linh Son Thon, district of the Thu Duc, province of Gia-Dinh.

For reasons still unknown to us, the local administration of Gia-Dinh has proceded to close our lodging-center. The former prisoners living at the center were arrested by the very public authorities who had earlier released them. High-school and university students who take part in our activities as well as benefactors who frequent our center with a view to helping the former detainees were arrested and beaten. Even three female monks bringing us rice were arrested.

To this day we have not been able to find out the reasons for the arrest of our lodgers and visitors.

We ask you, in your capacity as President of the Senate to intervene at once with the public authorities so that the three monks, the recently arrested high-school and university students belonging to our groups of social action, as well as the former prisoners arrested at this time, be released. We ask also that our lodging-center presently illegally occupied, be restored to us.

Chan Tin, priest
Committee for the Reform of
the Prison System of South Vietnam

Notes:

1) This letter is dated May 26, 1972, but no Saigon newspaper has dared to print it. Only the review DOI DIEN has reproduced it. Unfortunately, the distributing agency refused to take responsibility for this review. Moreover, those readers who receive it directly by mail find themselves subjected to intimidations of every sort. For all those reasons, the affair remains as yet unresolved.

2) Since the beginning of 1972, the Committee has been the object of a constantly violent repression.

1. Towards the end of February, 1972, the writer Thieu Son, a member of the presiding council of the Committee, was arrested and remains in prison to this day without news as to his condition. Thieu Son, more than 70 years old and very weak, could hardly walk at the time of his arrest.

2. M. Pham Trong Cau, another member of the presiding council of the Committee, 38 years old, lame, professor at the National Conservatory of Music, was arrested at his home on February 28th. It is still not known what has happened to him.
3. The parents of M. Pham Trong Cau, Mr. and Mrs. Pham Van Lang, aged respectively 72 and 66, were arrested the same day as their son while making a visit to the tomb of one of their daughters, victim of a plane accident caused by the Americans last year at Can Tho.
4. On March 17th, Professor Nguyen Van Trung, the R.P. Chan Tin, Mrs. Nguyen Long, the female monk Huynh Lien, M. Do Ngoc Long, and the superior monk Lieu Minh (members of the presiding council of the Committee) were summoned to the tribunal for having contacted the American Senator McGovern at the Redemptorist Convent at the time of his visit last year to Vietnam.
5. Professor Tran Tuan Nham, co-president of the Committee, a Catholic refugee from the North, a candidate in the senatorial elections of 1971, arrested on February 28, 1972. He is at present being held in Tan Hiep prison.
6. On July 27, 1972, Mr. Nguyen Long, co-president of the Committee, President of the Movement for the Self-Determination of the People, was sentenced by a military tribunal to 10 years detention and imprisoned at Chi Hoa for "having threatened national security."
7. Here is a list of students, all members of the Committee's secretariat, and all of whom have recently been arrested:

   1. Le Anh, student in the Faculty of Letters
   2. Cao Lap, medical student
   3. Lam Thi Ngoc Diep, a student at Gia Long High School (arrested on her way to the lodging center for former prisoners)
   4. Luong Kim Oanh, student in the Faculty of Letters (arrested under the same conditions)

C. Situation of Former Prisoners Previously Cared For in the Lodging Center

No.	Name	Age	Profile
1	Nguyen Van Thi	33	95% blind; nervous system ruined and stomach destroyed
2	Nguyen Tain	37	Heavy heart, abnormal pulse, General condition very serious frequent respiratory crises, and doctors in despair after over one year of treatment. A top heart surgeon could perhaps help.
3	Nguyen Thi Mam	19	Pulmonary tuberculosis for 2 years coughs blood. Right leg twisted during interrogation.
4	Nguyen Ngoc Ngam	32	1 leg amputated. Walks with crutches. Stomach disorders and fever.
5	Le Thanh Yen	23	Glandular tuberculosis. Swollen glands in ear and neck.
6	Nguyen Thi San		90% blind; stomach ulcer; indigestion.
7	Le Thanh Trung	34	Nervous crises and frequent muscular contractions as consequence of electricity shock interrogation. Crises last 10 minutes three times a day.
8	Nguyen Van Nam	55	Muscular rhumatism, nervous and violent headaches
9	Le Anh	30	Nervous system weakened. Suffers headaches and loss of memory. Pulmonary tuberculosis. Stomach disorders as a result of the breaking down of the nervous system.
10	Tran Van Long	26	Liver disorder. Rhumatism of the bones and muscles.
11	To Minh Tam	33	Rhumatism of bones and muscles; fever.
12	Nguyen Thi Hong	23	1 leg amputated. Generalized rhumatism.

APPENDIX H

FOURTEEN YEARS IMPRISONMENT

(Testimony of Mr. Nguyen Van Thanh before the October 1972 session of the International Commission of Enquiry into U.S. War Crimes in Indochina, chaired by Professor Gunnar Myrdal of Sweden. Mr. Thanh, 50 years old, comes from Hoai Than village, Hoai Nhon district, Binh Dinh province. He spent 14 years in jail, including 12 years on the Con Son prison island. Of these 12 years in detention on Con Son he was put into the Tiger Cages three times for a total period of seven years.)

Mr. Nguyen Van Thanh:

"I have been in prison for 14 years, 12 of these on Con Son island and three times in the tiger cages for a total length of seven years. I took part in the first resistance against the French. In 1954 when the armed forces, the people's armed forces, went North in regroupment, I as a non-military stayed back. I went back to my family to help rebuild after so many long years and started an ordinary persons life. Then, after some time, police, puppet army troops, "security guards" were sent by the Diem administration to surround my house and to arrest me. I was then sent from one prison to another, from the detention center of the district police, to the detention center of the provincial police and then to the provincial prison. During this period I was tortured many times. Then, finally, I was detained in an isolation cell."

"During the tortures and the interrogation sessions, I was forced to surrender, to renounce what I had done in the past. I thought I had not done anything wrong, so I did not surrender. Towards April 1957, I was brought to Nyan Than provincial jail. Then later I was sent to Con Son."

"I was brought to the island by ship. During the trip I had both my legs and my hands cuffed. When we prisoners came to the landing place on Con Son island, the guards pushed all of us into the water. A number of prisoners drowned. The rest helped each other to wade onto the bank. Then after that, the prisoners were assembled on a sand bank. The governor of the island, with a big stick in his hand, went from prisoner to prisoner and he beat one prisoner after another with his big stick. He threatened the newcomer prisoners with the following words: "This is not Con Son prison. We detain nobody here, this is Con Son hell-on-earth. If you surrender, then you may go back to the mainland. If you don't, then leave your bones here.""

"Then the prisoners were led to the cells through two rows of guards. Those with sticks and canes beat the prisoners whenever they went through the two rows of guards. We were put in block no. 1. Three days later, the interrogation began. They forced the prisoners to salute the Saigon flag, which you know is the flag coming down from the Bao Dai regime and of Thieu now. The prisoners were forced to renounce what they had done in the past, resistance and so on and so forth."

"We refused to salute that flag. We refused to renounce anything. Then we were put into dark cells, isolation cells. There was a room of about the same capacity as the room we are in now. Between 150-200 persons were detained in that room. Prisoners had to lie down on the cement floor. There were no blankets, no sleeping mats. Everyday prisoners on groups of 3-5 were led out of the room to be beaten. Our ration of food and drinking water was reduced time and time again. We had not enough drinking water. Not a single day passed without a group of prisoners being beaten. One day it was three, another day five, another day it was seven prisoners called to be beaten. The beatings occurred uninterruptedly. Apart from the beatings, there were other forms of terror. For instance, the prisoners would be locked inside that dark room for whole days to frighten them. Their rations of drinking water were reduced time and time again. With the shortage of food and drinking water and the lack of any fresh foods, vegetables for instance, many diseases occurred. From April to December 1957, the prisoners in block no.1 died one after another. I remember the figure for the dead during this period was about 300 from February to December 1957. From 1957 through '58 to '59 all of the prisoners in block no. 1, were detained inside the house. The number of deaths due to illness increased. Despite the fact that the number of deaths and the number of people stricken down by diseases increased, the prisoners continued to refuse to salute the Saigon flag. We kept struggling."

"Then towards the middle of 1959, the prisoners were one after another led to tiger cages. You have heard a lot about tiger cages. Tiger cages - what are they? Tiger cages are small cells of about 2 1/2 yards high by some 1 1/2 yards wide, that is less than the stretch of the arms of a grown-up. Now we were put into tiger-cages with no clothes on. Our legs were shackled, chained."

60

"Well, something about the tiger cages. The tiger cages were installed in rows. The walls were thick with a door in front of the cage. The ceiling was made of bars. There was a gangway between the rows of the tiger cages so that the guards could go back and forth along the path and supervise the prisoners below. The legs were chained to the walls. As for the hands, sometimes they were chained behind the prisoner. Other times, still they were chained together with the feet so that the prisoner had to bend down. In summer, a tiger cage would house 10, 12 or 15 prisoners. In winter the number of prisoners in each cell was reduced to 5 or even 3. Day after day the prisoners were taken out for beatings."

"There are different forms of beatings, by elbows, by fists, by knees. The brutes would thrust their knees or their elbows onto the bodies of the prisoners: in the chest, in the back and elsewhere. At times the prisoners had their legs and arms bound together and the whole body then pulled up to the ceiling. Then burning candles were placed under their feet, burning the flesh. The flesh would burn slowly, slowly. We had to do everything in the cage: eating, relieving ourselves. About the walking paths above the rows of tiger cages, the guard always kept either sacks of lime dust in powder form or lime mixed with dirty water, stinking water. Whenever the prisoners demanded anything either a few minutes out to have some fresh air or when the prisoners would shout to demand more food or enough drinking water, the guards would drop lime water or throw lime dust down upon the prisoners. It's suffocating. When we breathed in the air mixed with lime dust, it's very hot in the throat."

"As for food, the prisoners received each of them two small handfuls of rice every day with a can of water. You may know the size, a condensed milk can. There was a shortage of food, but never a shortage of beatings. Everyday, everyday, the prisoners were beaten. Many of them fainted, lost consciousness during the beatings. Prisoners were beaten simultaneously - in one cell, in another cell and in still another."

"On a winter night, whereas the prisoners had nothing on to serve as sleeping materials, the guards would pour cold water down upon the prisoners. Not only cold water, but cold lime water. After some time many of the prisoners lost their hair. Diseases were rampant and many died of illness. What kinds of diseases? Fever, typhoid, dysentery, pneumonia and heart diseases. Everyday there was some prisoner who died. One day there would be two, another three, another day five prisoners dying. The prisoners died with their hands and legs still in shackles. The dead would lie there in the cage from 9 or 10 in the evening until 11 or 12 o,clock the following day, until the guards would be so kind as to come and remove them. Whenever there was a dead prisoner in the tiger cage, the inmates would ask the guards to remove the·dead prisoners. But the guards would ask: "How many are dead?" If the answer was one or two dead, they would keep silent. They would wait until there were three or five dead then come and remove the bodies at the same time. Whenever a case of dysentery or typhoid fever would break out, the dead bodies would lie there for several hours on end. There would be stinking you know. The stinking liquid oozing out of their bodies and there were a lot of flies."

"This was harmful to the prisoners survival. Therefore, they demanded a little time outside. They were beaten for that. They were subjected to the pouring down of lime water, the spraying of lime dust. Sometimes, the guards used long sticks to strike down at the prisoners below, With more beatings there were more diseases and then more deaths. But more incensed became the hatred in the hearts of the prisoners."

"Tiger cages were so built that it was almost impossible for outsiders to know of it. There was only a small lane above open to the guards. Everything else was closed to outsiders. During the days we were in the tiger cages, we saw more and more prisoners being sent to tiger cages. These were prisoners who had been sent to do hard labor either to build roads or airfields. These were prisoners who for some reason or another were sent as punishment from the work detail to the tiger cages. Up to the end of 1959, about two years after I had been taken there, we moved apart from the seven blocks of cells. The Con Son prison also comprised two rows of tiger cages. My row consisted of 60 cages."

"Towards 1959 we got to know that there was a delegation of the International Red Cross who made a visit to Con Son island prison. But no one came to our tiger cages. As I have said, in Con Son when I was there, there were seven cellblocks and two rows of tiger cages. The number of prisoners who had their life laid down there was numerous, the cemeteries were abounding with new graves day after day - hundreds and thousands of them. That's all."

Hans-Goran Franck:

"Thank you very much for your important testimony. Questions?"

Prof. G. Favilli:

"I have a couple of questions. In the first place, do I understand correctly that your involvement in the resistance against the French was the sole reason for your detention?"

Nguyen Van Thanh:

"I never found out what was the exact reason for my being imprisoned. But like many others I did take part in the struggle against the French."

Prof. G. Favilli:

"Then you spoke of the effort to have you surrender as you said. What do you mean by "surrender"?"

Nguyen Van Thanh:

"First of all was their effort to compel us to salute their flag, the Saigon flag. Then an effort to compel us to renounce our faith in the revolution and later in the National Liberation Front. Also to obey every order they told is to do, to go build military projects, airfields and roads, or to public voice support for them. Of course being patriotic, we could not do such things as to speak ill of our resistance movement or to obey the orders they wanted us to obey."

Prof. G. Favilli:

"A third question. The guards of the tiger cages - were they Vietnamese or American? And the commanding officers - were they Vietnamese or Americans?"

Nguyen Van Thanh:

"The guards were Vietnamese. The functionaries were Vietnamese. The governor of the island and his aides were Vietnamese. But from time to time, we could see Americans in groups of three, or five - or twos or sevens coming perhaps from the mainland - strolling about the lane above the tiger cages.

Prof. G. Favilli:

"Final question to the present witness. Do you know, do you have any idea how many political prisoners there are at this moment in South Vietnam?"

Nguyen Van Thanh:

"For the time being, I don't know exactly. When I left the tiger cages in July 1969, the tiger cages and the cells were full of political prisoners. There were two types of political prisoners. One type of prisoner was detained there without any trial at all like myself. There were other political detainees who were kept there after some kind of trial.

Prof. G. Favilli:

"What is the criterion? Which people had some kind of court-martial and which had not?"

Nguyen Van Thanh:

"I don't know exactly the reason for their detention. But those are the facts. Those who had been brought there from 1959 - 1966 had some trial. Those who had been brought there before 1959 as myself had no trial at all."

Prof. L. Basso:

"First question, a point of clarification, The witness said that he never found out the exact reason for his detention. If I understand correctly the witness spent fourteen years in prison without a trial of any kind or a pronounced sentence?"

Nguyen Van Thanh:

"Throughout these 14 years, I was not even brought to trial a single time. It is not that my case is an isolated case. There are many prisoners there, who never knew any kind of trial at all."

Prof. L. Basso:

"Second question, I'd like to know about the Americans you heard outside visiting the prison. From what you said they never questioned the prisoners or sought information about their legal situation from [the time of] their arrest in Saigon?"

Nguyen Van Thanh:

"I remember one thing done by the Americans during their visiting tours. It happened to my cage. Usually we were chained in a kind of ordinary shackle made in the form of the number 8, where the legs and hands go through the two holes of the number 8. Then one day, three Americans came and inspected the shackles, the chains. First, they tried the door. They pushed the door to see if it was securely locked. They tried the chains and the cuffs. They showed signs of disagreement with these."

"A couple of days later, the number 8 cuffs were replaced by another kind of fetters. These new kinds of fetters. These new kinds of fetters had something like "In Good Will" with [word missing] on it. It is the kind of fetters that whenever the prisoners tried to move their legs, the fetters would lock further and further one step and yet another step through them.

Prof. L. Basso:

"I want to ask you, if in your opinion, the delegation from the Red Cross could have not discovered the tiger cages, of a complete investigation had been made?"

Nguyen Van Thanh:

"It is difficult for me to tell. What I do remember was that on the day we prisoners had to wait and wait for a very long time without being given the daily food and drinking water. Then we asked the guards and they replied: "Wait!" Now there is a delegation from the International Red Cross. They are somewhere but due to the fact that the only way leading to the tiger cages was blocked as a cover from outside, there is no way to bring food and water to you. We had to wait until night."

Prof. Joakim Israel:

"The Americans who inspected, were they in uniforms or in civilian clothes?"

Nguyen Van Thanh:

"I remember the three Americans in uniform. I didn't know their rank, but I heard some of the Vietnamese guards addressing one of the Americans as "Colonel", a colonel from USOM."

Dr. E. Agnoletti:

"At the last session of this Commission of Enquiry, Don Luce, an American, told how he came to discover the existence of the tiger cages. He confirmed that the Americans know about them. But he could not discover except by resorting to a sort of trick with two deputies [congressmen]. He said that there were tiger cages not only for men, but also for women. There have been a lot of women treated in the same way as the men. As for the Red Cross, I know that after the scandal of the tiger cages, the entire staff of the Red Cross in Saigon was changed. So in practice, it was recognized that maybe all that could have been done to discover their existence, had not been done. Especially after the testimony of Don Luce, the witness and members of the Commission will remember that in every prison and every interrogation center Americans were present."

Prof. E. Wulff:

"I direct my excuses for the next question to the witness, because after all we have from him, the answer seems to be obvious. But I want to ask it to make precise, nevertheless, whether he or any of his fellow prisoners ever received medical help, the help of a medical doctor in case of disease?"

Nguyen Van Thanh:

"Throughout all the years I was in the prisons and the tiger cages, I received not a single tablet of medicine. I remember once when there was a cellmate who suffered from some kind of typhus fever. We asked for medicine. The patient was given quinine instead. After taking the quinine, he got a higher temperature, a higher degree of fever."

Hans-Goran Franck:

"I have some questions too. Do you know where the equipment for torture or ill-treatment came from?"

Nguyen Van Thanh:

"These instruments for tortures and beatings: I don't know exactly about all of them. Many of them are of home origin, For instance, the sticks, the tables upon which the prisoners were forced down to have water poured down their mouths and the ropes by which the prisoners were hung from the ceiling as well as the buckets of dirty water they threw at us - these are of home origin. But the shackles, the fetters, and the handcuffs obviously of foreign origin. The handcuffs, for instance, had the words "Made in USA" on them."

Hans-Goran Franck:

"Have you seen any other equipment that comes from the United States, for example electronic equipment?"

Nguyen Van Thanh:

"There were many interrogation centers and detention centers in which there were electronic accummulators. These were of foreign origin."

Hans-Goran Franck:

"But can you say if some of them came from the United States?"

Nguyen Van Thanh:

"I don't know exactly if all of them are of American origin or not. But you know that in South Vietnam, all military equipment came from America and much of the electrical equipment captured did bear US markings."

Hans-Goran Franck:

"Do you know if the tiger cages still exist?''
Nguyen Van Thanh:

"When I left, there were still two rows of tiger cages. One row detained political prisoners who had had some kind of trial. Another row detained political prisoners who had had no trial at all. These two rows were parallel to each other. In fact, they stood back to back with a dividing wall in between and upon that wall was the walking lane of the guards."

Prof. E. Wulff:

"I apologize for this question. I'm sorry it's embarrassing, but I must ask it. How did you come to leave the tiger cages and Con Son island."

Nguyen Van Thanh:

"You have asked a question and I'm sure it's my obligation to find an answer. But in fact, it is difficult because my release was given no official reason at all. I guess, that one of the reasons might be that former resistance members like ourselves had been jeopardized for many years on end. In my case, it was fourteen years without a trial. Finally, it might have been impossible for the rulers to keep us as such quietly.

They released us. There were perhaps other reasons., perhaps due to the strong protest from people in South Vietnam against the harsh treatment of political prisoners. Perhaps it's also due to the strong movements of protest in the world. And also perhaps because more and more people were detained, more and more people were sent to Con Son island to the tiger cages. The rulers might have thought it better for them to release some of us."

Mrs. K. Fleron:

"Maybe this question ought to be the last one you should be asked here. Youll forgive me for asking. It seems to all of us a miracle or almost a miracle that you are still alive. I want to ask you about your health condition. Are you suffering from any diseases or weaknesses?"

Nguyen Van Thanh:

"I will try to answer your question, Madame. Of course it's difficult for us to remain still alive after the conditions in jail and so many tortures. I guess, perhaps, one of the things that helped me stay alive was that throughout the years, I was in prison, I kept telling myself that I must live - I must remain alive. Another reason might be is that before being detained, I was a rather robust guy in good health. The prisoners on Con Son composed a few verses of which the following is an extract:

> "Con Son is the kind of place to which it's easy to go
> From which it's difficult to leave.
> Those who don't leave their lives there
> Will return in a coffin."

The verse runs something like that.

Dr. E. Agnoletti:

"Does the witness have any knowledge about a contract signed by the American Marines, Department of the Navy, with a U.S. firm? We have seen the photostatic copy of this contract. The contract is for the construction of cells the same size as the tiger cages."

Nguyen Van Thanh:

"What I did know was that before 1958 or 1959 there were only five cellblocks. Towards 1959 two more cell-blocks were built under a contract with some American firm and with the participation of quite a few engineers from the Philippines."

Rev. E. Balducci:

"I would like to ask you if the prisoners locked in the cages had the possibility of seeking spiritual comfort or moral support, since this is a most fundamental right?"

Nguyen Van Thanh:

"We, the prisoners, did know that we had some rights for spiritual or moral support. But in fact, it is quite difficult to exercise this right. Whenever the prisoners demanded anything, then they would be sub-jected to brutal repression - to beatings, to the throwing or spraying of lime dust, to the pouring down of water so on and so forth."

Sen. E. Gruening:

"Did many of the prisoners die as a result of the beatings and the tortures inflicted upon them?"

Nguyen Van Thanh:

"Death as a result of beatings or torture is a very common event, in the tiger cages and on Con Son. The cases are many. I will recount only a few."

"One night during a period of a couple of hours, seven prisoners inside the tiger cages were beaten to death. They were later buried in a common grave in the sand dunes of Con Son. Their graves were still there when I left. I remember some other cases. In one case two prisoners were beaten to death immediately. There were two other cases in which a prisoner was beaten severely and died a half an hour later. There are many other cases of death as an indirect result of beatings and tortures and of the shortage of food and water. For instance, death as a result of diseases: Dysentery, typhoid fever, lung diseases, diseases of the liver and some other diseases which causes the prisoners muscles to retract so that they would gorge upon them-selves with their muscle retracted."

Sen. E. Gruening:

"Were there many prisoners who suffered permanent injuries such that they did not die right away but will have the injuries the rest of their lives?"

Nguyen Van Thanh:

"Such cases are many. For instance, though many prisoners were still alive when I was there, their nervous systems had been affected. From time to time there were prisoners who had nervous seizures. Some had either their arms or ribs broken or taken out. Recently, one member of the Commission asked about my present con-dition now. I thought I could avoid the question, since I don't think it's quite good to tell about my per-sonal condition right now. But since there is yet another question about the condition of the survivers, I think it is my obligation to tell of my condition just the same."

"First, my eyes have become weak. At times I find it quite difficult to see without glasses. My nervous system and my memory have been harmed. Sometimes, I can remember everything: other times, I just forget everything."

"The right side of my body still aches whenever I make a quick movement, especially when the weather turns. I have quite a number of scars still on my body. Of these scars there are two big one resulting from the burnings by candles of my flesh. They still ache."

Prof. I. Kende:

"I would just like to ask something about the profession of the witness. What did he do at the time he was arrested and put into prison?"

Nguyen Van Thanh"

"My village is an agricultural area. My family was a peasant family. I had remained a peasant up to the day I was arrested."

Chairman:

"I would like to thank you for your testimony, Mr. Nguyen Van Thanh."

APPENDIX I

LETTER FROM CON SON PRISON

June 1972

Dear Father...1/

Here is one of the saddest cases on which we have the duty to seek to alert, by any means, the conscience of mankind. This afternoon, I was passing by..., a camp under the command of my colleague..., a warden as I am. I was almost overturned with stupefaction by seeing there only women, some old people and more than fifty children under 9 years old. All these people came from Hue, Phu Cam, Phu Loc, Cau Hai. Some of the women were pregnant. All these people had no idea why they had been transported to the place where they are. In general, this is what happened: the officials of their commune took them to the commune offices for reasons not explained. While they were at the offices, the officials pretend they were taking them away as refugees and then they were transported to Con Son. They still do not know the exact reason for their deportation. I met an old woman with white hair. She told me she had 4 children, all in the Southern Army: 2 stationed at Saigon, 1 at Dalat and 1 in the 1st Military Region. She was brought here by force without knowing why. She wants to communicate with her children, but because she was deceived and forcibly taken away, she has not the KCB (Army postal address) of her children, so she no longer knows how to inform them.

...the number of these people totals about 1,500. I beseech you to collect clothing and money for them because, lied to as they were, they brought nothing with them. Two old women came wearing men's trousers...If you can obtain money, that would be even better.

I sign this letter clearly with my whole name so that I am not a stranger to you. I am certainly afraid of losing the means to feed my children, but my conscience will not leave me quiet, which is why I take the risk of writing to you. I do not fear that you will betray the secrets of your Ministry, but I am all too afraid that the letter may be discovered on route.

(name and address omitted)

1/

The dots (...) correspond to the names of persons, to places and to details which would identify the author of the letter, or which could jeopardise other people.

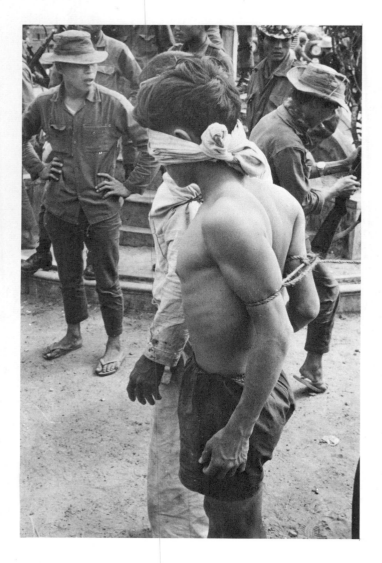

Binding and leading the
nine suspects to their
execution.

(PHOTOS BY DOUG HOSTETTER)

67

STATEMENT BY DOUG HOSTETTER ON EXECUTION OF SUSPECTS

During late January or early February 1968, large groups of civilians from the countryside marched into Saigon Government controlled villages and cities to demonstrate against the war. The villagers were unarmed except for some who carried bamboo sticks.

The District Chief at Thang Binh, located 30 miles south of Da Nang, was a North Vietnam Catholic refugee and militantly anti-NLF. When the demonstrators approached Thang Binh, he commanded his soldiers to mow down unarmed people.

The District Chief, Major Dang, told me that 300 "VC" had been killed in this incident. The American District Advisor reported that only two of those dead had been armed.

In response to this massacre, the NLF came into Thang Binh several nights later attacking the District Headquarters and inflicting some casualties. They then proceeded to burn a nearby Catholic refugee camp and killed over 40 people.

The District Chief had to save face with the villagers since the NLF had successfully attacked, sustaining no casualties of their own. On February 7th, the District Chief sent his soldiers into the countryside to take captives. Ten men were captured and brought into the District prison. There was no evidence that these were the men who had attacked the refugee camp, or that they were even NLF guerrillas. The only evidence, according to the American District Advisor, was that some of the captives were wearing webbed belts (easily available in the black market in any large village and often worn instead if the more expensive leather belts) which could have been used to carry hand grenades. One old man amongst the captured group was pardoned by the District Chief; the other nine were executed by firing squad in front of the village that same day. These photos show the nine men being tied up and led off to execution.

I happened to be in this village the day of the executions assisting a group of high school volunteers clean and repair the burned Catholic refugee camp.

Doug Hostetter
Vietnam Christian Service
1966 - 1969

APPENDIX K

UNDERMINING THE ANTI-COMMUNIST POTENTIAL OF THE PEOPLE

Mrs. Ngo Ba Thanh was a Professor of International Law at the University of Saigon. She has a PhD from Columbia University. In August, 1971 she was arrested after having participated in a demonstration protesting the one-man presidential election. No specific charges have been brought against her, but her lawyers said she was accused of having organized "an illegal organization," for having distributed printed material that "undermines the anti-communist potential of the people," and "for engaging in activities harmful to national security."

Thomas Fox, a correspondent for Dispatch News Service described her March 22, 1972 trial this way:

Shortly after arriving on a stretcher carried by military police to the regional military field court that tries "national security" cases, Thanh appeared to suffer an asthmatic attack, apparently brought on by the exhausting trip from the prison. She looked as if she were half her former weight. Her breathing grew rapid, while watching friends wept. Deputies who arrived at the scene minutes later in an ambulance injected Thanh with a heart stimulant after it appeared that her respiration and heart had stopped. The doctor administered artificial respiration, and women who crowded around the stretcher massaged Thanh's chest, hands, and feet.

With the fatigued woman still lying outside the courthouse, the doctor entered the court and testified before the five military judges that the woman's condition called for immediate medical attention. He demanded that she be released to go to a nearby civilian hospital, "the only one with the equipment necessary to aid Mrs. Thanh." He added that her condition was very serious, "her heart beat was up and down," and that "she could die at any moment."

The five judges recessed for 30 minutes before returning a verdict that the trial, would be postponed indefinitely, but that contrary to the doctor's request she could not go to the hospital but instead would be treated "with appropriate medical treatment" in Thu Duc prison. 1/

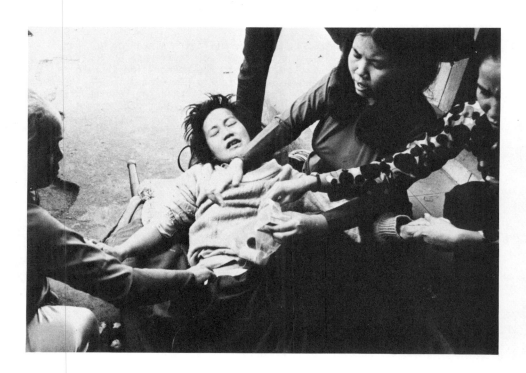

1/ American Report, April 7, 1972

(PHOTO BY DON LUCE)

Mrs. Ngo Ba Thanh (on right) a few weeks before her arrest. She is with a group who were in a sit-down strike at the National Assembly. They were protesting a decision of Tan Hiep prison officials, who refused to allow them to give food to their imprisoned relatives.

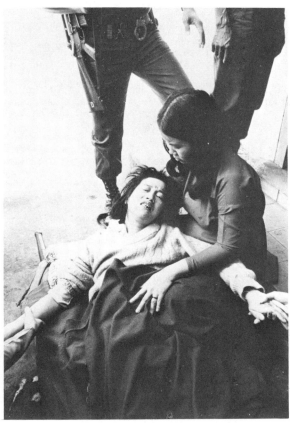
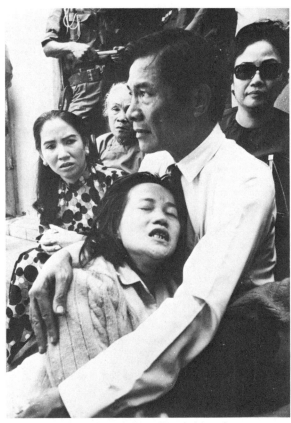

(PHOTOS BY TOM FOX)

Mrs. Thanh, several months later, at her military tribunal trial. At right, she is in the arms of her husband, whose request that she be admitted to a civilian hospital was denied.

THE BARBAROUS TORTURE AND BEATING OF WOMEN PRISONERS AT THE THU DUC PRISON

The beating and torture at the police stations and in prisons have existed over 100 years since our country lost its self-determination, independence and freedom. When a "suspected" communist is caught, beating and torture are considered a policy that helps the authorities carry out their purpose: That is, so-called "Inspecting" and "Re-Education." The policy still exists in the present time by the successive governments which protect their own interests and serve foreigners, disregarding the honor and the human values of the Vietnamese patriots.

Different Kinds Of Torture On Female Prisoners

Every torture bears in its nature a barbarous substance. Female prisoners, are unfortunately even more affected. Women are weak naturally and very sentimental, therefore, the ill-treatment may cause greater suffering to them. However, in spite of the profound mental and physical pain during the time they have been detained and questioned, all the female prisoners in Thu Duc have always believed strongly in the struggle of students from the universities and high schools and of people at every rank throughout the country. We understand fully that they struggle for justice and justice shall win though through many sacrifices. We all agree to offer ourselves for those who struggle for the country.

When we were captured and tortured, like previous prisoners, we had to endure these horrible punishments:

Clubbing

They blindfolded us, put our hands behind our back and pushed us down on the ground. A robust and drunken police took a club and beat our kneecaps, soles of our feet, head, shoulders, chest and back like beating into a stone mortar. While beating, they insulted is and obliged us to "confess" that we had liaison with the Communists. If we decided not to "confess" or not to know what we should confess, we were beaten until we were unconscious.

After being beaten about 2 hours, having fainted many times and recovered, a woman cannot rise up for her knees are weakened and swollen, black-and-blue welts cover her shoulders and back, blood from her head flows down, darkening her face. If she is beaten like that many times, it is inevitable that she can only crawl during the rest of her life.

In Thu Duc this terrible situation has been happening. Miss Que Lan, for example, a student of Faculty of Letters now exiled at Con Son, has been beaten so violently that her two legs are paralyzed and she has to use canes now.

Beating On The Soles Of The Feet

This kind of beating causes nephritis and damage to the victim's genital organs. Some women were beaten to death without any marks being left by the police. At the Central Police Service, we've heard that three high-school girl students were beaten to death but unfortunately we do not know the names of those 3 heroic students for we were not detained in the same cell.

Death in the concentration camp or in prisons is very often. The secret police and the Administration of the prison destroy their bodies immediately without reporting it to the family of the deceased. They usually keep the death secret to destroy the evidence.

Using Electricity

They usually attach electrodes to the weakest areas on a woman's body such as vulva, nipples, arm-pits, and tongue. This kind of torture causes some serious complications later. The attachment of electrodes to the vulva harms the uterus cells, without any medical treatment, the patient cannot have children. There are many women with lower-uterus illness now because of that kind of torture.

In addition, convulsions are also one of the consequences of the electrical torture: When having a fit, the patient's limbs are not in her control, she salivates, and sometimes cries out like a crazy person until she is unconscious.

In Thu Duc, the police even use the dual-wired electricity. Its consequence is more terrible. At night, lamentable screams escape from some concentration camps stirring emotions of those who have a little compassion and charity left in their hearts. However, the orderlies as well as the prison wardens never feel pity for them -- these laments are very familiar to them. Moreover, they don't have any emotions at all. They think that the victim's cries cause disorder in the jail, therefore, they scold them, they beat them more to keep them silent!

Dunking

Dunking is a very savage kind of torture, too. When water is poured into the nose and flows down and bloats the stomach, a paunchy policeman with his heavy boots, tramps on our stomach until the water flows out of our mouth. Because of this kind of torture, Mrs. Truong Thi Kim Lien has stomach trouble now. She cannot eat food and often vomits. They do not even refrain from tramping their boots on the belly of those in menstration or those who are pregnant. Therefore, the women very often have an abortion or hemorrhage after that.

Mrs. Truong Thi Kim Lien, for example, suffered a hemorrhage for two months. After being released, she was carefully taken care of by the students and improved gradually.

In the history of imprisonment in our country, there has never been a regime which causes as many abortions and hemorrhages as the present one.

Hanging From The Ceiling

The two hands of the woman are tied together and drawn up to the ceiling, the police then twirl her around, beating her until she is unconscious. To Nga, an eighteen-year-old girl student was beaten by this way many times at the First District Police Station during the night of March 5, 1970.

In general, the female prisoners have had to suffer many kinds of torture: pins put under their fingernails, pinchers or scissors used to cut their flesh, hitting their head agianst the wall, beating their back severly with a big stick. There are so many tortures and they are so terrible that we cannot state them all here.

In a female camp in Chi Hoa prison, Mrs. Hai, with a sentence of 15 years at hard labor, was beaten so severely that her backbone was broken. Now she cannot rise up and walk. Sentencing such an infirmed woman to 15 years at hard labor! Is this for the sake of charity by this regime?

While being beaten, the women are completely undressed. The orderlies used the most barbarous and cruel torture on the body: Putting pins into the nipples, the neck of a bottle into the vulva, extinguishing lighted cigarettes in some sensitive areas like the hip, arm-pits, thigh, neck...

Rape is accepted at the police stations and in prisons. Many women get sick or die after successive rape.

In addition, Mrs. Nguyen Thi Rieng had cloth rolled around her hand, then soaked with gasoline and set on fire until her hand was like carbon.

Sanitary Conditions

While being kept locked up in the cells, the women have only one set of clothes, no soap and not enough water. They are very wretched, especially in menstration period, when hemorrhaging or in uterus trouble. The sanitary conditions are even more limited to female prisoners at Con Son: Where can they get wash water when they have not enough to drink?

Separating Mother And Child

At the time of arresting the mother right in her house, the police oblige her to take along her children but they never let them stay beside their mother after they are already in jail. They send them to the police station and then take away the child and give it to some orphanage. This happened in the case of Mrs. Truong Thi Ki Lien. Her two-year-old child was sent to an orphanage. Two months later, when Mrs. Kim Lien was released, she searched for her child and found that he was mere skin and bones and could not stand up. Mrs. Tran Thi Hanh has been in Thu Duc jail more than two years yet she still has not been informed of the whereabouts of her 4-year-old child. Though she has asked for her son many times, the Administration of the prison has not given her an answer. Each service at the prison merely blames some other service for not having the information.

In another case, a mother captured in Trang Bom still does not know where her two little sons are and their situation at the present time. Terrorizing the women physically is not enough, they intend to terrorize them spiritually, separating mother and child, violating the women's virtue or beating them in front of their husbands. These are the most barbarous tortures. We demand the authorities to stop them all immediately.

The Imprisonment Policy Towards Female Prisoners

The Thu Duc Prison is largest female prison in South Vietnam. It is called "The Thu Duc Women's Reformatory," a very nice and humane label, however, the prisoners there consider it hell on earth because of its terrible cruelty.

Life of non-political prisoners (such as thieves, deceivers, thugs) is more agreeable. They live under easier conditions of eating, drinking, shopping and circulation. They often work in the office or maintain order while the political prisoners are moved from one camp to another. On contrary , the political prisoners have to suffer the regulations of a very severe administration.

Conditions Of Eating, Drinking and Shelter

The daily food ration was 29 piasters [less than ten cents] before April 15, 1970. After substracting the cost of rice and fire wood, only 5 piasters was left for meat and vegetables.

While we were still there, we heard that each person's share would be decreased following Mr. Thieu's austerity policy to serve the war. Our place was very humid, especially in the rainy season. Prisoners have to lie down on the moist floor month after month. The cell is narrow and crowded, the sick lying beside the healthy.

The more the government needs to "re-educate" the people, the more crowded the cells become. When there was not enough room for all to lie down, we had to share the small amount of space: One lied along the gutter, another on the path. In addition, the roof is so low that the heat is terrible and steam from the ground blows up. Moreover, malnutrition and lack of medicines help to cause and spread different diseases.

The Medical Problem

Permanent diseases are the consequence of torture, beating and the unhealthy conditions. Medicines are rarely given. When an Aspirin or Tyformycine pill is given, the sick person is already in a critical condition.

In fact, medicine is sufficient at Thu Duc prisons, Mr. Cam, a well-behaved nurse there said, but prisoners are not permitted to use it. This is one aspect of the present prison policy.

Mr. Tu is the only nurse at Thu Duc having the right to send a patient to the Doctor or hospital. Unfortunately, this nurse has no conscience, only resentment and wickedness. If moved to the infirmary, a patient is received most of the time with repeated complaints and insolent treatment. Usually she receives an injection of sedative, no matter what her sickness is.

All sickness claimed by the prisoners is considered false. Only when a woman is so weak that she cannot say anything does the nurse pay any attention to her. And then perhaps, he will send her to the hospital.

The Administration Of The Prison

Under the rule of warden Duong Ngoc Minh, the Thu Duc administration was the most brutal of all prisons. The prisoners had to endure an unbelievably wretched and painful life. Because of their struggle in August, 1969 demanding the body of a prisoner who was beaten to death, Duong Ngoc Minh ordered an increase in the repression. Four more were killed, suppressing completely the strugglers by sprinkling lime and spraying DDT into the cell. Three hundred prisoners were exiled to Con Son island. Day by day, Duong Ngoc Minh showed his intolerable cruelty and brutality by applying his "discipline." Prisoners were prevented from embroidering pigeons onto handkerchiefs, from singing or talking to each other, even though living in the same cell. They had to do hard work and line up to welcome high-ranking officers or guests even when sick.

They were not permitted to read newspapers or books including the history of Vietnam. (For the sake of charity, they started a school to teach the prisoners but prohibited the teaching of history. They were afraid that the female prisoners would follow the example of the historic heroes. They forget that the tradition of struggle remains everlasting in our people's blood).

Prisoners had to bow their head when meeting a high-ranking officer, salute the flag twice a day, stand upright while saluting, attend protestant services, disowning their own belief, absolutely obeying the regulations of the Center. If not, they were given the "discipline" system, which means the prisoners had to endure all the harsh tortures and severe beating described earlier and to lie in a dark, narrow, dirty room for a whole month while their arms and legs were shackled. They could not lie at full length. They could not receive relatives or bathe.

Under the control of Duong Ngoc Minh, there was a whole secret police system (made up of criminal prisoners usually). They mixed with the other prisoners to watch their attitude, their action and then reported to the security service. The more they reported, the more prisoners that would be punished and the more their own sentences would be mitigated. That is the reason why the secret police watch the prisoners closely and purposely harmed those whom they disliked.

Exploiting The Prisoners' Labor

There are some vocational training camps in the Center. Actually, these camps are only a place where the Administration uses the female prisoners' labor force brutally and inhumanly: In the sewing-machine training class, making an American military uniform returns only five piasters [about two cents] to the maker and two piasters for a mosquito net. The embroidering and knitting training class is opened to provide products for the Administration's exhibitions and then sold outside. Those who are skillful are sent to a warden's residence to work voluntarily. Those whose family is far away, try to work hard for some money. But when they fall sick and stop working, their names are registered. Three times like that and the Administration will apply "discipline."

Right Of Detention

Because there are so many regulations and so many secret policemen, the political prisoners are always being punished. Those who are sentenced with "bad conduct" (meaning breaking the Center's regulation intentionally or unintentionally) are kept by the Adminitration for unlimited periods of time.

One woman, almost 60 years old, excited one day because the next day she would be at the end of her sentence, was then called and informed: You'll be detained 6 months more for your "bad conduct" (because she once embroidered the figure of a pigeon and sent it to her family). Another was sentenced to one year imprisonment in 1959. However, as of April, 1970, she was still kept in the discipline cell because she dared to lead a movement asking for sufficient food, an end to hard labor, and refusal to attend Protestant services. The Administration considered her attitude "stubborn."

In Thu Duc, the prisoners are never released on time, they are usually kept at least six months beyond their sentence. Moreover, those who have suspended sentences or acquitted are still not allowed free, even the old and sick.

We must also mention here the tardiness of the secret service and the Military Field Court when investigating and preparing the dossiers. A person is kept almost 12 months in jail from the day of arrest to the day appearing in court.

By lengthening the waiting period, the Administration plans to wait for the sick and the wounded to be healed, leaving no marks on their body so that the evidence of their severe beating and torture in front of the so-called "justice" of the second Republic of Vietnam will disappear.

Why Are The Women Imprisoned?

Living in war-time and in a corrupt and unjust society like the present one, all Vietnamese feel pained and resentful at the collapse of all physical and spiritual values of the country. Who could have caused this terrible collapse except the foreign military forces? Since the foreign soldiers have landed their troops on this country, human values of the Vietnamese people in general and of the Vietnamese women particularly have been violated. How can we stay at home when our husband, our children, our relatives, and our friends are pushed into the bloody battlefields, sacrificed for a government which is so blood-thirsty, brutal, dictatorial and warlike? How can we stay home happily and watch our neighborhood spend an utmost painful life beside the intolerable luxury of those who betray their own people? How can we stay indifferent when hundreds of innocent girls are becoming prostitutes for money? How can we stay apathetic when looking at a girl's naked corpse lying across a barbed-wire fence encircling a U.S. military post or at a giant pile of garbage in front of a building or the headquarters of the allied soldiers?

In war-time, our life cannot be normal. All Vietnamese women hope to spend a simple and happy life in peace, but the present social situation of our country doesn't permit that.

Conscious of our responsibility to the national fate encourages the women to contribute in the struggle for human rights, independence and self-determination of the Vietnamese people.

Patriotism and the love of humanity of the Vietnamese women are the reasons for their arrest, detention and becoming the victims of all kinds of barbarous torture. They are innocent, indeed. When the nation is independent, when the spiritual values are determined clearly, those who beat and tortured them today will be condemned as criminals, history will condemn those barbarians who have leaned on foreign power over many years to threaten, terrorize and suppress their own people. It will condemn those who have killed so many Vietnamese, so many enthusiastic patriots.

The victorous independence and reunification of our country is prevented by their actions. Vietnam has been destroyed day by day, the people have endured many sufferings. All of this is the evident consequence of the infinite ambition of those who sell themselves to foreign powers.

Those Vietnamese who have little conscience and little patriotism left in this confused and worn-out society should listen to the complaints and screams of the prisoners during the night time all over they country. They should stand beside us to struggle for abolishing all the barbarous torture and the disappearance of so many prisoners. The Vietnamese should be released from the shackles, the tiger cages and the cattle cages that they have endured for so many years.

Saigon, August, 1970

Truong Thi Kim Lien
Vo Thi To Nga
Cao Thi Que Huong
Truong Hong Lien

A DENOUNCEMENT OF THE CRIMES COMMITTED BY THE WARDENS OF CHI HOA AND CON SON PRISONS

- a signed report smuggled out of Chi Hoa Prison

We, a number of women prisoners just transferred from Con Son prison to Chi Hoa prison on August 4th, denounce to the people the crimes of the blood-thirsty wardens, Lieng and Tuan, who repressed, beat, and sent us to Con Son as well as the crimes of Nguyen Van Ve, Nguyen Van Tran and their assistants at Con Son prison.

The killing of prisoners at midnight by Duong Ngoc Minh and his fellows at Thu Duc prison has stirred the people's attention. It was followed by the midnight repression of women prisoners at Chi Hoa and sending them to Con Son Island.

They sent us to Con Son because they did not want to answer our demands as they had promised on November 29, 1969. The demands were:

-- The release of the women without sentence or with expired sentence as well as the sick and crippled.

-- Not to beat and torture the prisoners.

-- To improve the conditions of prisoners.

At 12:00 midnight on November 29, 1969, when all of us were sound asleep, we suddenly heard the voice of Lieng (the director of Chi Hoa) speaking from a loudspeaker: "Pack your luggage and get ready to move to another place. You will find better conditions and comforts at the new place -- as I promised you before." Then he continued, "Military field police will help the women with packing, and will not beat the women." The voice of Lieng had just ceased when a shower of lime dust and tear gas fell upon us. Screams of protest and for help were raised. About a battalion of military field police, special trustees (military convicts) and about 200 civilian trustees (criminals) fully equipped with arms, and under the direction of wardens Lieng and Tuan and with the presence of officials from the Ministry of Interior, Police Headquarters, and the National Directorate of Corrections, took charge of taking us from Chi Hoa. Tam, the director of Tan Hiep jail, and a number of guards from Con Son prison got into our cells and repressed us. Bags of lime and cans of tear gas were thrown on us in the small cells full of prisoners. We were choked, our throats burned, some fainted and vomited blood. The blood-thirsty guards ran into the cells and beat us with clubs. They pulled us by our arms and hair, following the order "Three men try to drag one woman." Taking advantage of our confusion, the men barbarously beat us on our "female" places. We screamed more loudly in protest. Our bodies streamed with blood and wounds. Dragging us down the steps, they threw us one on top of the other and they even stepped on our bodies without pity. They also repressed the sick people at the clinical center. Even paralyzed women and a 60-year-old blind woman were beaten. Lime was also thrown on two of the babies who were about two months old. We thought they could not survive.

At the prison gate they threw us into the trucks like animals. Our bodies burned with bloody wounds mixed with lime dust. Our clothes were torn, some of us were naked. Some big trustees got into the truck and shackled us and threw more lime on us. While waiting at the airport, shackled, the trustees and military field police continued to beat us and throw more bags of lime. Then they threw us on the U.S. military planes. The Americans who saw it laughed in satisfaction.

We were dragged on our backs. The trustees pulled us by our arms and legs on the floor. Our bodies were swollen from the bruises. We were in rags rather than clothes. Our hair was tangled. At the Con Son airport, a trustee committee was waiting for the command of the major to "welcome" us. They said, "do you want to get on the trucks? We'll show you that this is Con Son Island, not the mainland." Immediately they threw themselves upon us and dragged us to the trucks ... and later we were thrown five at a time into the tiger cages. After taken all our belongings from our handkerchiefs to our medicine bottles (similar to Chinese Tiger Balm), our hair pins, our sanitary napkins ... they just left us a suit of our bodies in the midst of the cold weather of Con Son.

A tiger cage is five feet wide, ten feet long and eight feet high. The walls are of sixteen inch thick stones. Above us were the iron bars. In each cell there is a cement bench, 32 inches wide, six feet long and two feet high.

On the first day they gave us no food or water. On the next day each five of us received a paper "blanket" and each of us half a bowl of rice soup.

The life of the prisoners at Con Son is miserable. A handful of rice with some sauce full of sand and pebbles and rotten fish... The ration for one person is given to five. We were given three meals within seven hours and then we had to wait for seventeen hours without any food. We were given vegetables only four times in eight months. Only once were we given fresh rau muone (a leafy vegetable similar to spinach) which the Vietnamese never eat raw. These were given to us after terrible beatings by the "criminals" Ve and Tran. Now the women have no vegetables to eat.

We were not given enough food and drink. If we asked for more, they sometimes answered us by mixing our rice with petroleum, or mixing our dried rotten fish with soap, or giving us uncooked rice. We had stomach aches from these foods and when we were sick, they refused to give us rice soup. We denounced this to the nurses. When they were in a good mood they gave us some grains of salt for our rice soup. When not, we had to eat plain rice soup. Often they did not allow us to wash our bowls. So we had to eat out of dirty bowls on which the flies, dogs, and poultry stepped, or mice ran over. Rice was usually mixed with dust, the kind of dust that comes from the outdoor toilets through gusts of wind. We asked for clean bowls to eat out of. They hurried us: "if you eat slowly, we'll dump all your rice in one bowl and you'll have to eat like dogs from one bowl." Some women were sick and could not eat. They wanted to save their food, but their bowls were grabbed and the rice thrown away. "Next time, watch out," they were told.

The cells were narrow and hot. Five of us in one cell so we had to divide the space: two persons lay on the cement bench and three persons lay below, squeezed together like canned fish, the limited space occupied by the iron bars used to shackle us. One of us had to lie sideways close to the latrine bucket, with her legs bent day and night. Above our heads on the iron bars, there was always a barrel of lime dust. Each trustee had two rattan whips to lash us when they wanted. Wardens Ve and Tran allowed the trustee prisoners to place canvas beds over the iron bars where they could sleep and watch us day and night. They looked down through the iron bars and when they caught us going to the bathroom or changing our clothes they would purposely say, "feel at ease, we do not want to sit here, but we must follow orders." We protested against this to the chief of the cages, Mr. Nguyen Ngoc Nhan, but he said nothing.

Across from the tiger cages are the outdoor toilets which continuously send out bad smells. Each gust of wind brings the dust from the toilets and covers our hears, eyes and nose as well as our food and water. At night we could not sleep because of the cold, the mosquitos, our dirty clothes, thirst, and because of the trustees sleeping above our heads.

Each day they allowed us to empty our latrine bucket once. Just one of us was allowed to carry the bucket. Though the bucket did not contain much, it was heavy like a block of stone (because it is made of fresh wood and covered thickly with black asphalt). Because of our weak health, we tried hard to drag the bucket. If we happened to spill some of the contents, we were immediately punished. Sometimes when some of us got diarrhea or cholera, we asked them to let us empty the bucket immediately, but they refused. The bucket held three liters and sometimes we had to go to the bathroom in our basins. The narrow and hot cells always smelled of excrement and urine, sometimes mixed with the nauseous smell of the menstration which arises after 24 hours of being deprived from washing. For months, we only had a thin suit of clothes. We had to tear off our sleeves to use as sanitary napkins. Thanks to some who wore 2 pants at the time we came, we were able to have "mobile" pants to use and wash our pants. For months, each day we were only given a bucket of water to use to wash our faces and our sanitary bucket at the same time. In some cells, the prisoners had to leave the bucket unwashed or use a damp cloth to wipe out the bucket. When going to the bathroom, we tried to sneak a can of water to wash ourselves afterwards. Each time they caught us, they would swear at us: "You cows and buffalo women" or " you stone-eared women."

One mother who had a two-month-old baby could not feed him because she herself did not have enough to eat. Without water to wash the baby, she had to tear her clothes to wipe the baby. Without sanitation and through lack of food, the baby lost considerable weight and was seriously sick. Director Ve at that time felt obliged to send the baby back to the mainland. On his return to mainland, Dung's (the baby) eyes were rurny because of the lime that was thrown on him.

Each day when they opened the cell door, flies came into the cell in swarms. At night the bugs creeped all over the walls, and mosquitos made a kind of music flying around and sucking the prisoners' blood until the morning. There were thousands of mosquitos and bugs, their bellies swelling with the blood they sucked until they could not fly or creep anymore. Ants and worms also bit us, our bodies itched and we had festers from our scratching. Each week we were allowed to wash ourslves three times. Each time they gave us five minutes, time enough to quickly undress and pour one or two cans of water over our bodies. Sometimes before we could put our clothes on, the trustees would push the door open and come in with their whips, looking at us naked, swearing and kicking over the bucket and remaining water, not allowing us to contiue to wash our clothes.

When we were in menstration period, they only allowed us to wash our clothes once each 24 hours. And each time we must show the trustee the bloody water we wash our clothes with. The Vietnamese women are usually ashamed when they have to show to the trustees our dirty clothes in order to get permission to wash them. Without enough water and enough time to wash, we must cut our hair short or shave our heads completely. The Vietnamese women consider their long hair something very precious. Nhan and Sum, the top trustees, had some of the women shackled because "they (the women) disturb the peace by shaving their heads." The inadequate conditions at Con Son have caused many of us to suffer diseases such as: intestinal and stomach disorders, diarrhea, cholera, malaria, T.B., hemorr-hoids, typhoid, dropsy, paralysis, eye-disease, open wounds, and particularly a disease called "vomiting excrements" (because after months of being unable to go to the bathroom, and without medical treatment, we vomited the excrements). Through lack of medicine our diseases increased and we were transferred to the "clinics." When any of us fell in serious illness and when we called for emergency, not only did the trustees do nothing but they (especially Sum and Man) also threatened to throw more lime on us and swore:

"This is a cattle cage."
"These are brick and lime kilns."
"If you do not obey and if you keep demanding things, we'll give you more lime dust."
"Death is common in Con Son. If you die, we'll send you to the cemetary of Hang Duong."
"Medicine is given each ten days only. Don't ask for more."

One of the women had cholera and called for the nurses. However, not only did they not send any nurse down, but they accused her of being a "peace disturber" and shackled her arms and legs to an iron bar. So she lied there in the midst of the feces. The women must tear off their clothes to clean her. Not until she fainted did they take her to the dispensary. When a prisoner was too ill and had a brain attack (madness) Sum and Man ordered her shackled for disturbing order and took advantage of her situation to attack her body.

Each time there was someone sick in the cell and calling for medicine and a nurse, the trustees would come two or three days later to give medicine. When they arrived they would ask: "Is she dead?" In the morning the trustee would give medicine for three days, but in the afternoon when he came to inspect the cell, he would force the person to take all the medicine at once. Usually the patients which were carried away to the dispensary were paralyzed and in delirium.

The surface-cave", later used as a storehouse and now used as dispensary, is thirteen feet long, eleven feet wide and ten feet high. The roof is of tin sheets, the walls are of stone with only a 24 inch wide entrance. The cave is surrounded with barbed wire and there is always hemp sacks hung all around to hide it. This dispensary is close to the outdoor toilets. The prisoners must endure both the smell coming from the excrement and the burning heat in the hot season from April till June at Con Son.

The dispensary is like an airless cave, killing the women slowly. Each morning one would be heart-torn to see the paralyzed women crawling out of the cave to wash their faces. Sometimes out of exhaustion, some women fell down and lay there because the trustees did not allow anyone to help and take care of them.

Some women got appendicitis. But despite the doctor's proposing to send them back to Saigon for treatment, the trustees still made them suffer there. Whenever the women felt very painful and asked for the nurses, trustee Man would answer, "It's siesta time." Or Sum would say: "You can die here, we don't care. The only thing we care about is security."

The nurses took care of the patients in a very neglectful way. They used one needle for five patients and stole the medicine reserved for prisoners. As far as food was concerned at the dispensary, the patients received no better rations than the regular prisoners. Despite the doctors' recommendation to allow the prisoners to buy sugar and milk, the managers Ve and Tran still ignored the patient until she collapsed. Then they would give the patient a can of milk. When the old blind woman asked to buy some sugar to mix in her rice soup, Nhan violently answered: "I don't care about your old age. I don't care about your being sick."

The women's life became more miserable because of the crude theft of the trustees. A month after our arrival at Con Son, through repeated demands, they finally gave us some of the belongings that we brought along from Chi Hoa. Our clothes, medicine, food, all the belongings that our families had brought to us with their sweat and tears, the trustees had piled them all together in a stack. In the rain and sun they stank and looked like a pile of garbage in the city. Flies and bugs gathered around these belongings and we tried to take what remained from the pile. Yet they still threatened us to prevent us from taking these things, so that they could steal them easily. Nhan and Ba Chau (the head of the trustees) and the other trustees tried to steal everything they could from the prisoners. On Christmas Eve, while the women were lying cold and hungry in the tiger cages, the trustees organized a "festival" with the food and other things stolen from us. They took all the precious items, leaving the things that were unimportant. Mixed with lime and urine, the rest of our belongings became rotten. If we tried to dry them out in the sun, the trustees would come and punish us. They told us they saved our food; however later the food disappeared. They stole every little thing from us when they pretended to inspect our rooms. They would take a pin, a nylon bag, a bit of salt, a tablet of medicine, even a belt. The acts of theft by the trustee Sum went on without notice thanks to the protection of Ve, Tran, and Nhan. Within eight months, we were allowed only once to buy food and medicine. However, right after our purchase, they came to inspect the cells and took everything: salt, pepper, sugar, medicine... During these eight months, none of us were allowed to see our relatives or correspond with them. Packages sent to us by our families were opened by the trustees for "inspection" and "security." All the food items were then stolen...salt, sugar, pepper, canned food. If we made claims, they would answer: "Stop asking for them." They also stole the gifts that people sent. They would only give some part, and take the rest, for instance the cloth sent to us by the Buddhist monk, Venerable Nguyen Thanh.

In the eight months we were twice repressed with lime dust. The first time was on the fourth day of Tet, the most sacred day in Vietnamese tradition. During these days we were not only not allowed to enjoy Tet, but also the trustees ordered by Ve and Nhan decided not to open the cell gates to give the women some freedom. They even found reasons for the trustees to beat the patients in the dispensary. While the patients were washing themselves, they hurried them and kicked the water over. They used the bars of the cell door to beat us without mercy. Some of us still bear wounds to the present day. Some vomited blood. Because of such scenes, all the women protested. They were immediately repressed with lime. During that Tet holiday, prisoners in other cells were also repressed for other reasons.

The second time occured on April 28, 1970. When the women cried out when they heard cries of protest coming from the men's tiger cages, Nhan and Sum, shirtless, shouted: "I give orders to throw lime on them until they die." The trustees rushed towards us, throwing bags and buckets of lime upon us which had been set on the iron bars above. Buckets of water followed. We were choked and burned by the lime mixed with the water. Many fainted, others vomited blood. One woman was seriously injured when a block of hard lime fell upon her head. At the same time they went into the dispensary and threw lime onto the patients four times until all of them collapsed. Despite that, they stuck the rest of the lime into the nose, mouth and eyes of the patients so that some were blinded, other vomited and coughed out blood. After the repression, our bodies as well as our belongings were all covered with lime. Yet they did not allow us to wash ourselves and clean the cells. So for two months, we kept lying in the lime. We did not have a bit of water to cool ourselves. We must wash our clothes with urine, consequently we itched and were covered with wounds. Because of the intense heat, we only wore underclothes.

At these times Ve and Tran and their American "master" would go over the iron bars and watch us below like people watching animals at the zoo.

We were punished for very absurd reasons such as chatting too loudly in the cell, or asking for drinking water, bringing water into the cell to wash ourselves after going to the bathroom, wearing underclothes because of the heat and the lack of clothes... We were punished from one week to one month by not being allowed to wash our clothes, bodies and faces. Nhan and Sum often ordered the trustees to stir up the buckets of lime or just open the cover so that the wind would blow gusts of lime dust down on us. Sometimes Sum would even scatter the lime along the way above the cells. If we protested, "don't you think it's enough to punish us? Do you still have to throw more lime?" Sum would threaten us: "Who said that? Watch out my child!" All through eight months, we continued to hear dirty swearings, threats of Sum, Man, Nhan...even the director, Ve, would use dirty language when talking to us.

The policy of using prisoners to rule other prisoners is a most evil method of the prison chief. Particularly at Con Son, military culprits and common criminals are used to rule over other prisoners. To prevent the emotional weaknesses of the trustees, the prison chief ordered that those that symathize with political prisoners would receive 200 lashes, or go to the stone cave to chop wood, or be shackled. Unable to suffer these physical punishments, a number of prisoners followed orders and beat other prisoners.

On August 3rd, they returned 108 of us to the mainland including the seriously sick prisoners from the dispensary. On board the Con Son ship, many collapsed and vomited blood. They brought along 50 trustees to beat us. After some gunshots (because the women refused to be shackled) and after the repression, many of us fainted and coughed blood.

The beating of prisoners is very common in the jails of South Viet Nam as well as the sending of women to Con Son Island for torture by the managers Tran and Ve. The harsh treatment, the stealing, and the continuous insecurity of the prisoners in the jails, especially at Con Son Island, are more inhumane than under Hitler's regime.

Not only the healthy women prisoners, but also sick prisoners brought from Con Son to Chi Hoa, were beaten by the trustees under the order of Loi Nguyen Tan (Chi Hoa warden). Our bodies are covered with bruises because we dared to speak out when they took one of us to another cell.

After fifteen days back in Chi Hoa, we asked the manager-Committee to solve our main demands such as allowing contacts between the prisoners and their relatives and improving the prisoners' conditions. They promised to do these things, but afterwards left our demands unsolved. On August 8th, Loi Nguyen Tan ordered the trustees to come into the cells and beat us with clubs, table-legs, iron bars, and iron wheels. Only when blood had streamed enough did he order his puppets to stop. After this repression, four of us were wounded, one seriously.

Talking about the prison, one cannot forget Camp 5 of Cho Quan hospital. This is the central hospital of the South Vietnamese government to treat the serious cases sent by the various jails. However it is the place where one can legally destroy the evidence of violent repression, beatings, assassinations by the interrogation agencies and the various prisons. They can easily say that the prisoner died of sickness. Quan, the cruel chief nurse is nothing more than an authoritative policeman who has the right to refuse serious cases of illness sent to him from the island.

These are only the partial facts about the cruelty of Con Son and Chi Hoa prisons. Realizing that:
- the denial of freedom of thought is against international law.
- the detention of prisoners without sentence or with expired sentence, of crippled and chronically sick prisoners is an illegal act.
- the torture, beating and ill-treatment of prisoners is an act of blood-thirsty fascists.
- the act of leaving the prisoners in thirst and hunger, not giving them adequate medicine, killing them slowly is an inhumane act.
- the disrespect of the prisoners' human rights, treating the prisoners as if they were animals, the vulgar swearings, and the punishments are violations of human rights.
- the use of prisoners to rule other prisoners is a crude act of the thiefs.
- the denial of relationship between the prisoner and his family, between the prisoner and his fellow is an act against human morals.

We, the women prisoners, denounce the repression, the beatings, the killing, and the violation of the prisoners' dignity by Nguyen Van Ve, Nguyen Van Tran, Pham Van Lieng, Pham Ngoc Tuan, Loi Nguyen Tan, and the others, the wardens of Chi Hoa and the slaughterhouse of Con Son including: Danh (Chi Hoa trustee), Chin Khuong (Con Son trustee) Nguyen Ngoc Nhan (Camp Chief at Con Son), Nguyen Minh Chau ("reformer" at Con Son) and all the blood-thirsty trustees - Nghi (Chi Hoa trustee), Ba Chau, Sum, Man, Sang, Ne, Phat, Lap, Phu ....

-- We strongly protest against the Ministry of Interior, Police Headquarters, and the Directorate of Corrections which have given orders to the managers of the prisons to terrorize, repress, beat, and shackle the prisoners and send them to Con Son prison.

-- We ask the Committee for Prisoners' Relation, Women's Committee for Human Rights, Saigon Student Union and all other organizations to denounce the cruel acts and crimes of these people in front of the people in the country and throughout the world..

-- We ask that our demands be presented to the authoritative offices of South Viet Nam to solve the following points:

1. Freedom of thought and ideals of the prisoners must be respected.

2. The prisoners' lives must be guaranteed. Women prisoners' dignity should be respected. Prisoners should not be beaten, tortured, repressed or shackled.

3. Prisoners' conditions should be improved: food and drink and medicine should be adequately given to the prisoners. The cells should have more space and prisoners should be allowed to do reading publicaly .

4. Women prisoners without trial, with expired sentences, crippled and sick prisoners should be released.

5. The "criminals" causing bloodshed and their fellows should be thoroughly punished.

6. Con Son prison system should be abolished.

7. The 185 women prisoners presently in Con Son prison should be immediately returned to the mainland.

8. Packages and checks and other belongings stolen from the prisoners should be repaid.

9. Family relations of the prisoners should be allowed regular time for visits and plenty of time for care should be given.

We put all our faith in you and impatiently wait for your intervention to denounce the false democracy, the illegal beatings, terrorism and the inhumane treatment of the authorities which has given such bad consequence to us.

Chi Hoa, September 20, 1970

A number of women returning
from the Island.

We enclose the list of names and signatures of 82 of us. The others are scattered all over in other jails and are not here to sign.

Nguyen-thi-Man	Nguyen-Ngoc-De	Nguyen-thi-Sau	Nguyen-thi-Tam
Nguyen-thi-Hue	Tran-thi-Binh	Huynh-thi-Gai	Doan-thi-Luan
Nguyen-thi-Phi	Nguyen-thi-Ba	Banh-Duong	Huynh-Ngoc-Anh
Ngo-thi-Ba	Dang-thi-Bon	Lam-Xuan-Bao	Nguyen-thi-Thanh
Vo-thi-Ba	Dao-thi-Tuyen	Le-thi-Diep	Bui-thi-Ba
Pham-Xuan-Hoa	Pham-thi-Minh-Hong	Nguyen-thi-Moi	Tran-thi-Sau
Nguyen-thi-Hai	Tran-thi My-Phuong-Dung	Nguyen-thi-Xuoc	Nguyen-Kim-Huong
Huynh-thi-Hoang	Ngo-thi-Nam	Nguyen-thi-Chung	Tran-thi-Ha
Ngo-thi-Boi	Tran-thi-Lau	Nguyen-thi-Tra	Tran-thi-To
Huynh-thi-Muoi	Pham-thi-Hien	Nguyen-thi-Phung	Nguyen-thi-Phe
Pham-Le-Nao	Le-thi-Hue	Ton-thi-Anh	Ho-thi-Ut
Nguyen-thi-Lien	Pham-thi Thu-Ba	Huynh-thi-Dau	Nguyen-thi-Kheo
Nguyen-thi-Hoa	Nguyen-thi-Thuc	Vuong-thi-Vui	Trinh-Thu-Nga
Nguyen-thi-Chuyen	Nguyen-thi-Muoi	Nguyen-thi-Phuc	Vo-thi-Anh
Huynh-Thuy-Minh	Tran-thi-Thoa	Nguyen-thi-Dung	Lo-thi-Chinh
Vo-thi-Thanh	Le-thi-Liem	Nguyen-thi-Be	
Nguyen-thi-Nga	Nguyen-thi-Huynh	Nguyen-thi-Be	
Nguyen-thi-Loi	Nguyen-thi-Hanh	Nguyen-thi-Bay	
Pham-thi-Bai	Nguyen-thi-Anh	Nguyen-thi-Hue	
Le-thi-Cuon	Nguyen-thi-Dao	Tran-thi-Ty	
Nguyen-thi-Ba	Nguyen-thi-Vang	Phan-thi-Chinh	

APPENDIX N

INTERVIEW WITH A THU DUC PRISON OFFICIAL ABOUT CONDITIONS IN THAT JAIL

Interviewer's Note: *The following account was given by an official at the Thu Duc prison whose name cannot be included here because it would endanger his life. This official's account was verified by official at the Ministry of Interior in Saigon, by letters smuggled out of Thu Duc prison, and by interviews with released prisoners......Don Luce*

On the night of August 21, 1969, Duong Ngoc Minh, Director of the Thu Duc Correction Center ordered 13 women punished. The women were on fast to protest the frequent beatings given them.

Dang thi Ranh, 16 years old, and Nguyen thi Tan, 41 years old, were beaten first. After this, they were put in the Catholic Church inside the prison while the other eleven were beaten. Then the wardens returned to Ranh and Tan.

The two women were forced onto the floor and beaten separately. While each woman was forced to lay on her stomach, Warden Ha Quy sat on the woman's back and pulled both legs up to a vertical position. Then Warden Le Van Nhan beat the soles of the women's feet with a club.

The two women had been on a fast for five days in protest to previous beatings. Their bodies were covered with black-and-blue bruises from the waist down.

The prison director, Duong Ngoc Minh, directed the torture while his wife stood by his side and kibitzed. Warden Ha Quy had refused to participate in any of the previous beatings, but according to people who were at Thu Duc at that time, Minh "forced Quy to assist in the torture of Ranh and Tan."

After the beating, the two women were taken to a large cell holding about 100 women prisoners. Here the women's representative council made up of prisoners inside the cell refused to accept the two women. They saw that the situation of these two was very serious and told the guards to take them somewhere else. They pleaded with the guards to give them medical attention.

The guards then returned and told this to prison director Minh, adding that they thought the situation was very dangerous. Minh was reported as replying, "Put them in. It will make the prisoners afraid."

Two hours later Ranh and Tan died. All of the women inside the cell began crying and calling out. Their voices were heard by the people in the houses around the jail beginning at about three a.m. on the morning of August 22nd.

Prison Director Minh became afraid and asked the women for the two bodies. The women inside, however, refused to give up this evidence of the prison administration's cruelty. Minh organized all of the soldiers, the wardens and the women trustees (criminal prisoners and prostitutes) to go in and get the bodies.

After obtaining the bodies by the use of this force, Minh took them in a car to Cho Quan hospital in Saigon. His idea was to get the doctor to say that they died from sickness. The doctor at Cho Quan refused to do this and sent them back to Thu Duc where they were put into the rice warehouse.

Then the medical doctor for the Thu Duc prison, Captain Khanh, filled out papers stating that Ranh and Tan died from heart disease and T.B.

For the next two days, the women took turns calling out to the people of Thu Duc: "They have killed our sisters. They have beaten to death Dang thi Ranh and Nguyen thi Tan. We have no food and water. Come and save us." Director Minh, in an attempt to end the women's protest, had shut off all food and water to the prisoners.

On August 23rd, the assistant prosecutor from Saigon came to Thu Duc to make an investigation. He refused to accept the certificates of death and ordered the Thu Duc police to have a public health doctor examine the bodies. The new doctor, named Toai, and the prosecutor were reportedly paid off with 200,000 piasters [more than 1500 U.S. dollars at the official exchange rate] each. Dr. Khanh's death certificates were accepted and the bodies of Dang thi Ranh and Nguyen thi Tan were buried quietly.

Late evening, August 23, 1969, a third woman, Nguyen thi Xuan Dao, died. Mrs. Xuan Dao, around 40 years old, had been part of the earlier five-day protest, had been beaten several times, and was further weakened by Director Minh's policy of cutting off all food and water to the women to end their protest. Her death was simply recorded as due to "sickness."

After Mrs. Xuan Dao's death, the prison authorities decided to send the most active women to Chi Hoa prison in Saigon. The warden from Chi Hoa, Colonel Lien, talked with the prisoners and persuaded them that the case of the killings would be brought before a court of justice. Only then did the women agree to leave Thu Duc. More than 300 were then sent to Chi Hoa prison in Saigon about 15 miles away.

Repression continued at Thu Duc. Minh, apparently afraid word of the killings would get out, told the women he would do even stronger things. About 100 of the women were shackled, five or six in a tiny room. They were also beaten, though not as badly as before.

The women who were sent to Chi Hoa prison continued to demand a trial for the murderers of Ranh and Tan. Afraid that news would leak out, the prison authorities decided to send the women to Con Son prison in late October, 1969.

When they were told that they were being sent to Con Son prison, the women refused to leave. When the prison guards tried to come into the cells to pull them out, the women threw their buckets of excrement at the guards. It was only when tear gas was used that the women could be controlled and the authorities could get them to the airport where they were sent to Con Son by an American plane.

At Con Son, the women continued to resist the authorities. They would not enter the prison gate. The Con Son authorities called about 100 trustees (criminal prisoners put in charge of the other prisoners, mostly political at Con Son) to help get the women into the prison. The male trustees were all naked to "scare the women." The frightened women ran into the prison and were locked up in the Tiger Cages.

APPENDIX O

WOMEN PRISONERS WHO ARE SERIOUSLY ILL MENTALLY

(Editorial Note: The following list of people was prepared by the Committee for the Improvement of Prisons in South Vietnam and dated May, 1971.)

1. Chi Nguyen thi Que, 45 years old, arrested in November 1959, has mental trouble as the result of suppression and torture in the prison. She was sentenced to 10 years' imprisonment, and was moved from one prison to another - Thu Duc, Chi Hoa, Phu Loi and all the prison administrators know that she is a mental case. But for more than 11 years already she has been in prison and no care is taken for her health.

   Her husband died in 1967 and her daughter was killed during bombing in 1968. Now she is still in the prison of Chi Hoa.

2. Chi Nguyen thi Phe, 35 years' old, arrested on August 3rd, 1963 and sentenced to 5 years' imprisonment. Her home town is far away in Binh-Dinh and her son, 3 years old was taken care of by other people. The poor child, without a father or mother, cared for by others, died after several months.

   Thi Phe has serious stomach trouble, for which on care is taken. She has been given injections of Atropine and is becoming blind. Even the German doctors in the prison of Con Dao saw that her condition was serious and suggested that she should be moved to the mainland for treatment. Today, her period of imprisonment has been exceeded by 2 years and 7 months, and her condition becomes more and more serious, but the government does not agree to her release.

   She is still in the prison of Chi Hoa.

3. Chi Nguyen thi Xuoc, 45 years old, arrested in 1962. Her home district is Binh-Dinh. She was arrested with her son, 11 years old. After several months of investigation, her son was released. He wandered about in Saigon, and after 8 years she does not know if her son is alive of dead, or if he may have returned to Binh-Dinh.

   As the result of torture and the dampness of the prison, today her lungs are affected and she is given no treatment.

   She was sentenced to 4 years imprisonment, but today, she has served already for 8 years. The day of her release, when she hopes to see her mother and her son, is still far away.

4. Chi Ton thi Anh, 47 years old, arrested in Binh-Dinh on July 26th, 1961. She was sentenced to 7 years' imprisonment. Now she has TB and stomach trouble and no care is taken of her so that she cannot walk, nor eat and drink properly. For the last two years the government refuse to release her.

   She is still in Chi Hoa prison.

5. Chi Nguyen thi Kheo, 36 years old, was arrested in 1960, in An-giang. In the local prison she was tortured so that she vomited blood and was moved to the hospital. When an attempt was made to force her to sign a false confession, and she refused, she was again beaten by the police.

   She was unmarried when sentenced at 26 years of age to 7 years' imprisonment. Today, she has been in prison for more than 10 years and the government does not agree to release her, although an official in Thu Duc prison told her in 1964 that her sentence has been reduced by 1 year. During the 10 years she has been moved to all the prisons in the south: An-giang, Chi Hoa, Phu Loi, Go cong, Thu Duc, Phu Loi, Con Dao, and now is the third time she returns to Chi Hoa.

   No competent doctor has diagnosed her illness - she is very weak and thin and old-looking and menstration has ceased.

6. <u>Chi Nguyen thi Thao</u>, 47 years old, arrested on May 2nd, 1960 and sentenced to 10 years imprisonment, when her daughter was just 7 months old. During the time of investigation she was moved from prison to prison: Gia Dinh, Chi Hoa, Phu Loi, Thu Duc, Con Dao and back to Chi Hoa. She tried hard to keep the child with her, because she did not want her to be sent to an orphanage. After hearing from her family, she sent the child to her sister, but unhappily her sister died. The child was then sent to the grandparents who also died. For ten years the little girl has wandered from house to house in the village, without family affection and without education, showing how corrupt South Vietnamese society has become.

    In August 1970, thi Thao was taken from Con Dao to Chi Hoa and was able to see her daughter, who cried: "Mother, do not die, you have to live with me. Your sentence is finished, why are you not released? Do the administrators of the prisons not have any children? Why do they not know how to love children who have no mothers?"

    But thi Thao cannot hear - she has become deaf.

    She has TB, but the prison nurse always gives her quinine. So that, after ten years in prison, the TB is very advanced and the deafness is extremely serious.

    The day of release and the reunion of mother and daughter is far away.

These are some cases among the 83 women prisoners now in Chi Hoa. They are proof that the prisons of South Vietnam today are savage and inhuman and must be reformed.

APPENDIX P

ARE SAIGON STUDENTS BEING TORTURED?

(Editorial Note: This is a translation of a front-page story in TIN SANG (Morning News) newspaper, April 11, 1970. TIN SANG was confiscated because of this article and has since been closed down entirely. The April 24, 1970 Baltimore Sun contains a detailed article on the torture of these same students.)

On April 9th, the Field Court's magistrates queried all the students presently held in the Saigon reform center. During the hearing, all students denounced beatings, interrogations and barbaric activities, such as clubbing with truncheons and pieces of teakwood, shocks with electric current, tortures using soapy water forced into the nostrils and ears and using fire and oil to burn the genitals and chest. They said mind-dimming drugs were also used. In addition, the students said Metropolitan Police and First District police used false documents, signatures and testimonies to prove student's guilt.

Take the following case of Huynh Tan Mam [tr. note: Mam is the acting chairman of the Saigon Students Union imprisoned since March 20th] as an example.

Mam was beaten with truncheons on the knees and hit (all over) until his body was swollen. He was also threatened with water-electric shock treatment.

From the day he arrived at Metropolitan Police Headquarters, Mam has been interrogated everyday from midnight until six in the morning. A testimony Mam gave in front of the interrogators and the director of the police station was not presented for examination. Instead a false declaration which was read to Mam quickly at five o'clock the morning of March 30th was used. Despite the extreme methods used against him, Mam has stuck to his original story.

Mam has not signed anything, despite the fact he was sent to the hospital and police headquarters three times to be made semi-conscious by drugs in order to get him to sign.

The Case of Thanh,Hoa,Son

In the presence of the magistrates, students Thang, Hoa and Son retracted their signatures from a statement incriminating Mam which they signed during interrogations.

The Case of Student Do Huu But

He was shocked with electricity, beaten with truncheons and tortured with soapy water forced up his nose in order to get him to admit he had relation with student Duong Van Day. But at present is in shock. He cannot walk and screams at night.

The Case of Do Huu Ung

He has been interrogated the most of any. His penis, pubic hair and chest were covered with oil and scorched by flame. His knees were beaten until soft and water poured on them to cause infection. His body is black-and-blue. Electricity and soapy water have also been used on him. Needles were forced under his fingernails and a truncheon broken on him in attempts to get him to sign a prepared statement for the Metropolitan Police.

The Case of Vo Ba

He was beaten on his knee caps and beaten between the fingers. Electricity was also used on him. Having tricked him into signing a statement, the interrogator beat him cruely when he asked to see what he had signed.

The Case of Nguyen Tan Tai

Electricity, anesthesia, soapy water and truncheons were used on him. Presently he lies unconscious with a weak pulse. He could die any time. Tai was asked to sign a statement saying it was true the police had found weapons and explosives kept at his house, even though he was not at home [at the time of the search] and though the statement contained incorrect names of his father, mother, brothers and sisters.

The Case of Nguyen Thanh Cong

His wife's aunt, pregnant with child, was beaten in front of him and the security personnel threatened to strike her genitals to cause a miscarriage in order to get him to sign [a confession].

The Case of Duong Van Day

Soapy water was put in his ears, his ears then beaten, He is now deaf in one ear, which also drains blood and pus. Nor can he hear clearly from the other ear. His two legs are paralyzed. He cannot stand or walk. Of these students most seriously beaten (But, Khiem, Tai, Day), all of whom are now confined to beds, he was the most severely beaten. Anesthesia was also used on him.

The Case of Tran Khiem

He is in about the same condition as the other three most severely beaten. He has been sent to two hospitals. His two legs are paralyzed and his knees show little reflex. He is confined to bed. He has not signed anything.

The Case of Nguyen Ngoc Phuong

His right leg was beaten to the point it is now immobile. His wife, Cao Thi Que Huong, was also beaten to the point where she could not walk unassisted. Secret police threatened to strip her naked and drag her off if he did not sign a statement.

The Cases of Students Nguyen Ngoc Yen, Phung Huu Tran, Ho Nghia, Le Hoang Thao

The situation of these students is similar to those above but they are all still able to walk .

APPENDIX Q

THE TORTURE OF UNIVERSITY AND HIGH SCHOOL STUDENTS

Chi Hoa, June 12, 1972

Dear Father:

Up to this afternoon, the total of university and high school students arrested is more than a hundred and among them we know about 70 by name. The majority are still held at the Headquarters of the Municipal Police. All have been savagely tortured. All have had to be carried on stretchers to their cells after interrogation. Electric torture, forced drinking of soapy water, the implanting of needles in the tips of ten fingers - these are the current methods. The condition of the students now at the Headquarters of the Municipal Police is scarcely different to that of the students at the National Institute of Agronomy two years ago. Miss Nguyen Thi Yen, after a night of torture on June 9, 1972, lay unconscious. The student, Trinh Dinh Banh could neither walk, nor eat. The police had to spill milk on him forcing open his mouth. The student Vo Thi Bach Tuyet had small mice and lizards dropped on her body. All this has been reported by students who saw these deeds with their own eyes and who have just been transferred from the Municipal Police Headquarters to Chi Hoa. Taking advantage of the confusion due to the military situation and, in consequence, of the present absence of public interest in the student problems, the government has increased its arrests, its repression and its more and more savage torture.

So far as the 30 university and high school students at Chi Hoa are concerned, the government intends to deport them to the prison island of Con Son. Not long ago, the Venerable Nguyen Van Nai, one of the students arrested during the campaign against the election of the single candidate Nguyen Van Thieu was deported to Con Son without any trial.

We know that there will be university and high school students on the next boat leaving for the island. Even the families of imprisoned students have suffered repression. On the morning of June 9, 1972, two relatives coming to see students were arrested at the prison gate and imprisoned. It was even a security officer of the prison who provided that information and perhaps in a few days we will have more details.

Faced with these repressive measures, with imprisonment and with torture, we entreat you to ask leaders of the churches to intervene, if possible, by raising their voices, in the hope of being able to restrain the acts of the government. We ask you to protest in the press, and to ask other priests and teachers, especially Professor Trung and Father Can to write articles in our defence. Because of our difficult circumstances, we cannot write to all our teachers, and if you are able to see them, please give them our greetings. We hope with all our hearts that you will do everything possible at this time to help us. As for the future, shall we be still at Chi Hoa, able to write to you occasionally? Or shall we lie in the tiger cages of Con Son listening to the howling of the waves and seeing only four walls of the prison, imagining that they are the walls of our Faculty lecture rooms?

Dear Father, accept our warmest wishes for your good health.

(name and signature omitted)

(Editorial Note: These descriptions were smuggled out of prison in June, 1972 by prisoners to a groups of Catholic priests in Saigon. A similar report may be found in the August 13, 1972 issue of the New York Times)

University and high school students have been savagely tortured. Interrogation takes place usually during the night, between 10 o'clock in the evening and 2 or 3 o'clock in the morning.

We list below some typical treatment used on students we know; similar treatment has been used on a great number of others whose names we do not know.

The Student, Nguyen Thi Yen

Treasurer of the General Association of Students of Saigon, arrested on June 8, 1972. She was beaten until she lost consciousness, made to stand upright with no clothing on before 10 torturers. Her nipples were burned with lighted cigarettes.

The Student, Trinh Dinh Ban

Chairman of the South Vietnamese Federation of Students. He was beaten until his face bloated, his eyes wounded and infected so that he can no longer see clearly, the ends of his fingers were pierced with needles, his chest and the soles of his feet were beaten. He is now unable to walk.

The Student, Vo Thi Bach Tuyet

Vice-Chairman in charge of relations with the Committee of the Struggle of the People for the Right to Life. She was beaten for several weeks on end, and was then suspended by her feet in the air, together with another student, for several weeks in a dungeon very brightly lit, with small mice and ants dropped on her body. She was then imprisoned in a flooded dungeon.

The Student, Nguyen Van Nam

Vice-Chairman of the above Committee, in charge of internal affairs. The same treatment as the student Trinh Dinh Ban cited above, but in addition, he was given electrical torture and had his fingers contorted with rods, so that they are now paralysed.

The Student, Nguyen Thi Hue

Chairman of the Association of Buddhist Students of Saigon. He was injected with chemicals (thruth drugs?) for several days, and was then forced to sign a report after such an injection.

The Treatment Inflicted On The Students

The university and high school students now imprisoned at the General Headquarters of the Municipal Police are for the most part in a very bad state of health because of the tortures.

The food is insufficient - each meal consists of only a half bowl of rice and a few pieces of dry, spoiled fish.

Families are forbidden to visit their children in prison or bring them food.

As of now, the students are completely exhausted and frequently lose consciousness.

(name and signiture withheld)

PLEASE TO INVESTIGATE THIS TRAGIC NEWS

New: "Theo nguồn tin thông thạo, ngày 24.1.71, chánh phủ Saigon đã đổi nhà số 107/22 Trần quốc Toản Saigon bắt giữ hai đứa con trai của một cán-bộ Mặt Trận Giải Phóng Miền Nam (NLF) tên Tư Minh, Tư lệnh Biệt Đội Đặc Công Saigon - Cholon (nhà báo Công Luận số 933 ra ngày 31.1.71 đã đăng.)

Ngày nói trên, hai đứa con trai tên Nguyễn văn Quý sanh tháng 4 1965 và Nguyễn văn Huy sanh tháng 12/1966 đã bị bắt giữ cùng với người chủ nhà nuôi con tháng. Được biết thêm chánh phủ Saigon bắt giữ 2 đứa con của Tư Minh làm con tin chánh trị nhằm mục đích dụ hàng. Nếu Tư Minh không ra hàng, chánh phủ Saigon sẽ cho thủ tiêu 2 đứa trẻ ấy."

dear Mr. Dean,

    Please to investigate and translate this tragic news. I need you to publish this urgent to stop this government from cruel. My friend said your good man to do this. Please to hurry.

                                    thanks,
                                    Hai

Translation: According to the news of January 24, 1971, the Saigon government came to house number 107/22 Tran Quoc Toan, Saigon and arrested the two children of an NLF cadre, Tu Minh (reported in the Cong Luan newspaper number 933 of January 31, 1971).

The two children, Nguyen Van Quy born in April 1965 and Nguyen Van Huy born in December 1966, were arrested with the person who took care of them.

The reason that the Saigon government arrested the two children was to use them as political hostages to entice Tu Minh to defect. If Tu Minh does not defect, the Saigon government will eliminate these two young children.

APPENDIX S

PEACEFUL HAPPY NEW YEAR

A CALL FOR PEACE -- FROM THE IMPRISONED MONKS IN SOUTH VIET NAM

From the dark, narrow and filthy cells, we five hundred imprisoned monks in South Vietnam, urgently send this call for peace to all good will people working to stop the war in Vietnam.

We consider this our duty, firstly because we have opposed this inhuman war by nature since the beginning; and secondly because we are suffering all kinds of ill-treating solely because we refuse to bear arms against our own brothers.

We are monks and taoists belonging to the great and popular religions of Vietnam such as Buddhism, Caodaism and Dao Dua; but above all, we are followers of the greatest and most popular religion in Vietnam - and we believe throughout the world - that is the religion of Peace. We prefer imprisonment to murder and our ideal reflects that of the majority of the Vietnamese people, especially the peasants who suffer the heaviest calamities in this war.

Since 1960 at the onset of this war, thousands of our monks and taoists have courageously chosen the prison as non-violent (ahimser) fighters for Peace. As the war escalates, our hardships multiply. Many of us have been killed in insecure areas, withered miserably in the cells and "tiger cages", and waiting hopelessly for more than 5 years behind the bars.....

The South Vietnamese authorities do not recognize the conscientious objector's status of our religious vocation. Before May 1970 we were prosecuted at the Front Court-Martial as political prisoners with the maximum penalty without revocation. After that date, the Front Court-Martial being judged anti-constitutional by the Supreme Court, we are brought before the military court as simple soldiers convicted of "civil disobedience" and "disobedience to higher orders" (articles 105 and 116, Military Code 1951).

With the same so-called offense, we are sentenced again and again, and shuffled from the induction center to the prison through the court; and we become perpetual prisoners. The purpose of the government is to terrorize us and to demoralize those peace-loving young men who want to follow our examples - by refusing and abandoning the war.

On November 1st and December 1st, 1970, we have celebrated two 10-day fastings to denounce the above injustice:

 We demand:

1. That those monks and taoists who have been sentenced by the anti-constitutional Front Court-Martial must be set free or re-judged before a civil court.

2. That those monks and taoists who have completed their terms of "civil disobedience" must be released from prison to return to their pagodas.

To demonstrate to the government our determination against the war, our love of peace and our defense of religious freedom - 50 (fifty) persons from among us have opposed the forceful draft and life-long imprisonment imposed on our monks and taoists by self-destroying our eyes, limbs and fingers. Those people want to make themselves unfit for manslaughter for life as a sacrifice to their religious ideal. We are ready to go up to harakiri and self-immolation to awake the government against its religious oppression. We rather voluntarily give up a part of or the whole of our bodies than to inflict a damage on the lives of our brothers.

On this occasion of Christmas and New Year we raise this call for peace to inform the public about the injustice we are undergoing, to give witness to peace-loving people the faith that love and peace will overcome hatred and war. At last, we solemnly burn the incense, close our hands and pray for all a PEACEFUL HAPPY NEW YEAR (we cannot have any happiness unless we have peace). Please have the kindness to pray with us.

Made at Saigon Military Prison - December 21, 1970

Bikkhu Thich Nguyen Nhu, Badge No. 57283, Buddhist Representative

Dang Van Hung, Badge No. 60376, Caodaist

Nguyen Hong Long, Badge No. 60638, Dao Dua Representative

APPENDIX T

MASS ARRESTS OF BUDDHISTS

VIETNAMESE UNIFIED BUDDHIST CHURCH
Institute for the Dissemination of the Dharma
    COMMISSION GENERAL FOR YOUTH

Saigon, May 26, 1972

To the Association of Vietnamese Students in France:

The Vietnamese Buddhist Students Association in Saigon solemnly and urgently informs the entire Vietnamese student population, all overseas Vietnamese students groups, and all friendly student organizations in the world of the increased repression against organizations that are for peace in this Southern part of Vietnam.

Under martial law the Saigon authorities have so far arrested the following:

1) The student Trinh Dinh Ban (President of the Federation of University Students in South Vietnam), Vo Nhu Lanh (President of the Van Hanh University Student Union), Tran Thi Hue (National Affairs Assistant Director of the Saigon Buddhist Student Association) and hundreds of other students whose names have not yet been ascertained.

2) The entire Representative Body of the Faculty of Letters student body has been arrested except for its chairman, Lam Ba Phat, who is still at large.

3) The entire Representative Body of the Faculty of Sciences student body has been arrested.

4) The entire Catholic Youth Worker Union.

5) The entire Committee to Struggle for the Right to Life.

6) The Committee for the Betterment of the Prison Regime in South Vietnam.

7) Some 170 students from the Minh Mang student campus.

At present time secret police are searching for the rest of those not yet arrested and the homes of Buddhist students in Saigon are being occupied day and night by the secret police. A number of those arrested have been sent to the prison island Con Son without having had any trial.

Solemnly and urgently,

In unity,

Nguyen Phuong Danh
President, Buddhist Student Association

APPENDIX U

LETTER TO YOUNG CATHOLIC WORKERS (YCW) INTERNATIONAL

Saigon, July 3, 1972

Dear Friends:

As you know, in the middle of the night of April 30/ May 1, 1972, the Saigon police came and searched the central office of the YCW and arrested all the young people living there, that is:

> 9 young workers between 15 and 16 years old;
> 2 school pupils of 17 years old;
> 5 members of the YCW National Committee, including the Chairman, Nguyen Viet Tuan.

Nguyen Viet Tuan, a teacher in a public primary school, 23 years old, does not usually sleep at the central offices. But on that day he had to work very late getting ready for the Work Festivals, and he stayed there overnight. As an official, he was little involved outside his professional work and his own activities in the movement. As for the other members of the national committee arrested during the night April 30/ May 1, they are busy among the young people of that circle. So the police could not find precise charges against them. That is shown by the fact that after their arrest, they remained in the hands of the police for two months. Through various vigorous steps, we asked for one thing only: that if charges could be brought against them, the affair should come to court; if not, that they be freed immediately.

One May 15th, a delegation of 8 chaplins went to the Police Prefecture to try to obtain news of them. The Chief of the Special Police, who is responsible for such arrests, informed us in all seriousness that the matter of our young people has been remitted to the Court Martial, and that it was to the Court Martial that we should go to get the information we wanted.

We approached not only the Court Martial but also the Civil Court of Saigon, the only two competent judiciaries in Saigon. The Court Martial replied in writing on May 18th, that after examining all their reports and minutes, they could find no trace of this affair; on May 19th, the Civil Court of Saigon told us the same, orally.

At the Police Prefecture, they refused once again to see us and did not reply to our letters demanding an explanation. However, after June 12th, our friends again appeared on the list of detainees at the Police Prefecture authorised to receive food from their families. From this, we were informed of the place where out friends were detained. No one has yet been able to get in contact with them. But people who have been detained with them at the Police Prefecture, tell us that they have been very badly mistreated, that many of them have been badly tortured; Nguyen Viet Tuan, our Chairman, and Doan Khac Xuyen, a member of the National Committee, have been living nearly a month in the dungeons.

This is the situation of our friends in prison. The offices of the YCW remain under police surveillance. No activity is possible in Saigon. Many of the leaders still have to hide. Recently released from prison with the VIDOPIN workers, we have been without news of Vu Si Hung, another member of the National Committee for nearly a month: we don't know whether he was arrested or not. For in Vietnam there exist all too many organizations who can make arrests and such arrests are not always made with a judge's or police mandate, very often by abduction. This is why it is very difficult or even impossible to get information.

We are not the only ones to be treated like this. Hundreds of young people have been arrested and interned for months and months without being tried; thousands of men and women of all kinds and of all ages are being deported to the penitentiary of Con Son and their associates and families do not know why.....

Father Truong Ba Can
YCW Chaplain for South Vietnam,
370 rue Le van Duyet, Saigon 3.

APPENDIX V

DECLARATION OF TWELVE PRIESTS

(Editorial Note: The statement below, signed by twelve Catholic priests was translated from the August 1972 issue
of Doi Dien (Face to Face), a Catholic monthly in Saigon. On October 17th, Father Chan Tin,
editor of Doi Dien and a leader of the Young Catholic Workers, was sentenced to five years in
solitary confinement by a military court in Saigon. He was charged with publishing articles con-
sidered "Communist propaganda and detrimental to the national security.

We the undersigned priests unanimously feel that:

1. For a long time the government authorities here, in the capitol as well as in the provinces, have ceaselessly
   applied a policy of terrorism: indiscriminate arrest and internment; especially during these last two months
   the government authorities have taken advantage of difficult circumstances to step up the intensity of this
   policy of terrorism.

   A. Arrests are more nearly carried out as kidnappings. Rarely is there a proper warrant for arrest. People
       are imprisoned but no one is told where. People are imprisoned for an unlimited time without trial.
   B. Not only in all the prisons on the mainland but also on the island of Con Son there are prisoners of every
       kind: the old, the young, pregnant women, the sick and disabled.
   C. Although the Supreme Court has acknowledged that agencies of the government have engaged in torture and
       meted out such punishments, the government not only never charges, it has recently increased the intensity
       of this policy with the arrests of high school and university students.

2. The above policy is in complete contradiction not only with the constitution but even more with the very
   basic demands of human rights. Not to mention the spirit of the Good News as specially proclaimed by the
   Second Ecumenical Council of the Vatican in the Pastorial Constitution on the Church in the Modern World, paragraphs 27 and 28.

3. In any circumstances, even under martial law or in a situation of tension, all rights of man and woman must
   always be respected.

   Because domestic public opinion has been silenced by the policy mentioned above, we raise our voices to alert
   public opinion in the entire world and especially before the conscience of those who call themselves Christians.

   This policy in the southern part of Viet Nam as well as in other countries on the side of the Americans has
   proved now more than ever: the term "Free World" is only a deceitful lie of American imperialism and those
   governments created by the Americans.

   Saigon, July 4, 1972

Rev. Chan Tin   Rev. Tran The Luan
Rev. Truong Ba Can   Rev. Nguyen Nghi
Rev. Bui Thong Giao   Rev. Huynh Cong Minh
Rev. Vu Xuan Hieu   Rev. Nguyen Van Phan
Rev. Nguyen Viet Khai   Rev. Phan Khac Tu
Rev. Nguyen Nguyen Ngoc Lan   Rev. Nguyen Huy Lich

APPENDIX W

TO REPORT TRUTHFULLY

Reports and Letters from the Quaker Team in Quang Ngai Province, Vietnam, 1972
(Collected by NARMIC, a project of The American Friends Service Committee, 160 North 15th Street,
Philadelphia, Pa. 19102)

Since 1968 the Quaker Service Team in Quang Ngai Province of South Vietnam has paid frequent visits to the local prison and the prison ward of the province hospital. Besides attending urgent medical needs, they have distributed medicines regularly to patients with long term problems and provided an infant feeding program (canned milk, soap, vitamins) for children jailed with their mothers. In July, 1970 Dr. Marjorie Nelson gave testimony to the House Sub-Committee on Government Operations of the evidence of maltreatment and torture she and other members of the Team had observed. In July, 1972 Marge Nelson is remembered by a 35-year old woman in the hospital ward; a Team member observes: "Marge goes home and testifies before Congress about the torturing she witnessed at the prison, but the same woman who was tortured four years ago is still in prison and still being tortured and no one has done a damned thing about it." For years the Team has witnessed first-hand the effects of torture, and more recently, an increase in its use. In August, 1972, one member of the Team wrote to the home office of the AFSC in Philadelphia, "the police repression due to the new martial law and the mass numbers of people being arrested and tortured is at an all time high in Vietnam" and urged, "We should report truthfully and in detail what we know about this situation in the same manner we report civilian war casualties."

The main job of the Quaker Team has been to operate since 1967 a Rehabilitation Center, which is supported by the American Friends Service Committee. Free medical and nursing care, physical therapy and artificial limbs are provided each year to over 800 people, without regard to religion, political views or income, though the Center accepts only civilians for treatment. Soldiers and veterans are given priority at other rehabilitation centers. About 80% of the patients treated at the Center are old men, women and children.

Two themes especially have filled the letters from the Quaker Team in Quang Ngai to the Philadelphia office: anguish at the U.S. government's insistence in pursuing the war and prolonging the suffering, and admiration for the courage, spirit and ingenuity of the patients and staff at the Center. About three-quarters of the patients have war-caused injuries. In 1971 the Team issued a statistical summary which reported, "Of those patients willing to state clearly which party in the war caused their injury 69% placed responsibility with the Allied forces (U.S. and ARVN) and 31% indicated that the NLF caused their injuries."

With similar care the Team has recorded their experiences with the prison: To report truthfully. Following are reports of the Quaker Team of their recent (1972) knowledge of treatment of prisoners. Some of the letters discuss the difficulties the Team have encountered in their dealings with prison authorities, both Vietnamese and American. In April Team visits to the province prison were stopped. In August the Team received a letter from a province official expressing some regret that he could no longer approve of work which served only to heal the enemy.

Correspondence and reports from Quang Ngai are dated and numbered according to the Philadelphia AFSC office filing system. To protect people who might suffer retaliation from the authorities, names are changed.

The first document was prepared in October, 1972 by Jane and David Barton, Field Directors, Quaker Service, Quang Ngai, and is "an overall impression" from the AFSC staff and medical personnel who have examined prisoners. Following this summary, reports and quotes from letters are presented in chronological order. To protect people who might suffer retaliation from the authorities, patient/prisoner names are changed.

Report from the Field Directors, Quaker Service, Quang Ngai

PRISON CONDITIONS, QUANG NGAI, VIETNAM, OCTOBER 1972

For the past five years the American Friends Service Committee doctors and team members in Quang Ngai have made medical visits to the Quang Ngai Prison. There has also been a diet supplement program for women being detained with their young children. Medical visits have also been carried out at the prison ward of the Quang Ngai Province Hospital. At the same time many prisoners requiring surgery, prostheses, and physical therapy have been referred to our Rehabilitation Center for treatment. Due to this involvement with the prison situation in Quang Ngai, American Friends Service Committee team members have been able to gather many first-hand accounts from Vietnamese people who have been confined, interrogated, and tortured. American Friends Service Committee doctors and medical personnel have examined many patient/prisoners whose injuries appear to be directly related to the tortures they describe.

The following information was gathered from first-hand reports of prisoners and from observations made by AFSC staff in Quang Ngai concerning conditions of confinement, interrogation, and torture at the Province Interrogation Center, the Quang Ngai Prison, and the prison ward of the Quang Ngai Province Hospital:

1. Prisoners explained that during interrogation they were forced to drink large amounts of water mixed with whitewash (lime), soap, or salty fish sauce. When their stomachs became bloated, the interrogator jumped on their stomachs. One AFSC doctor examined several patients who had "petit mal" seizures and memory lapses. He felt this was due to brain damage caused by the drinking of such toxic material.

2. Prisoners also told an AFSC doctor that they were often forced to lie on a table and if a prisoner didn't respond to questioning properly, the interrogator would reach underneath his rib-cage and crack or break the prisoner's ribs. This same doctor examined and had x-ray evidence of several prisoner/patients with cracked or broken ribs.

3. AFSC doctors have examined many prisoners who have complained of internal aches and pains. These prisoners often had black and blue marks, open wounds, and raw skin showing on their bodies. The prisoners claimed the injuries were caused by general beatings to their bodies — especially to the back of their necks, bottoms of their feet, and chest — with club-like sticks. For instance, on two occasions an AFSC doctor examined prisoners with chest injuries. The prison officials claimed these two prisoners had fallen down a well, but the prisoners told our doctor that they had in fact been beaten.

4. AFSC doctors have witnessed prisoners, as many as fifteen women, having emotional fits or seizures. The prisoners convulse violently, froth at the mouth, and have muscle spasms. Other prisoners try to tie their arms and legs to some stable object and hold the convulsing prisoners down so that they won't hurt themselves. One doctor witnessed as many as five prisoners convulsing, thrashing, and yelling at the same time. These fits or seizures greatly puzzled AFSC doctors who had never seen similar seizures in the United States. AFSC doctors suspected that these prisoners had experienced emotional trauma and that these seizures were either an emotional release or a subconscious attempt to avoid further interrogation and torture. Two AFSC doctors have witnessed prisoners having hysterical reactions when electric lights were turned on in the room where they were allowed to examine the prisoners. Later it was reported that these prisoners had been tortured with electricity.

5. Prisoners have claimed that during interrogation police have molested them and hit them when they would not respond to questioning. One such case is that of Nguyen thi Lang* who was interrogated for nine hours before losing consciousness. When she regained consciousness her vagina was bleeding and continued to do so for several days. Afterwards, our medical staff treated her for hysterical fits. Then she was taken from the prison ward at the hospital back to the Interrogation Center where she says the interrogators banged her head repeatedly against a wall. Examination later of her x-ray by our medical staff showed a skull fracture and brain hemorrhage. As a result, John Talmadge diagnosed that this prisoner "suffers from persistent right-sided hemiplegia and, in addition, she manifests symptoms of a complex neurological disorder." He requested that this prisoner be transferred from the prison to the hospital for treatment but no action has been taken by the prison authorities.

6. As a result of confinement, many prisoners have contracted tuberculosis. These prisoners are rarely given any medical care. In fact, our doctors have seen many cases which they were not allowed to treat. The doctors have also noted that these prisoners were not isolated from the others, so that there was and still is much communication of TB among the prisoners.

7. The medical care given to prisoners at the Quang Ngai Interrogation Center, Quang Ngai Prison, and prison ward of the Quang Ngai Province Hospital is almost non-existent. No Vietnamese doctor or trained medical person sees any of the prisoners and there are few medicines stronger than aspirin available. In the past the AFSC doctor was allowed to make weekly visits to the Quang Ngai Prison but could examine only those patients the prison officials wished the doctor to see. The AFSC has never been allowed to visit any prisoners at the Province Interrogation Center but patient/prisoners from the Interrogation Center have been treated when they come to the prison ward of the hospital. Our doctors have had no control over the patient/prisoner's length of stay in the prison ward and many of them have been returned for further interrogation even though they were still diagnosed as seriously ill and under treatment. One example is that of Pham thi Tho*, whom our medical staff discovered had a

---

*See Notes on Some Prisoners Treated . . . for more information and statement of medical staff.

94

"definite and unmistakable irregularity in the rhythm of her heart" which was symptomatic of a cardiovascular problem of potentially serious consequences. In addition the patient had a three-month old fractured femur due to a bullet wound and thus was unable to walk. Our medical staff wanted to remove the bullet from this prisoner's leg and to evaluate properly the cause of her serious heart condition, but the prisoner was returned to the prison and he was unable to treat her. In efforts to treat patients at the Province Interrogation Center, Quang Ngai Prison, and the prison ward of the hospital, the AFSC staff has continually been thwarted by a lack of cooperation and humanitarian concern on the part of the Saigon government and the American advisors.

8. Prisoners who are at the Quang Ngai Province Hospital for treatment are chained to their beds by prison guards regardless of their injury. In the prison ward of the hospital patients are chained two together as well as to the bed. There they are released twice daily to hobble together to the bathroom. Three patients receiving treatment at the AFSC's Rehabilitation Center - a paraplegic, an above-knee amputee, and a fractured femur case - were all handcuffed to their beds for periods of a year and a half to two years without knowing why nor by whom they were being held captive. They had never been to the Province Interrogation Center nor to the Quang Ngai Prison. The history of their arrivals at the hospital followed a similar pattern. They were all injured in "insecure" areas, taken to the American military hospital at ChuLai for emergency treatment, then moved to the Quang Ngai Province Hospital at which time they were immediately chained or handcuffed to their beds and never questioned by police or government personnel. Proper medical care, physical therapy, and prosthetic care for these prisoner/patients were severely hindered and their recovery prolonged by this practice of handcuffing and chaining them to their beds.

The Province Interrogation Center is located in Quang Ngai city but is a separate facility from the Quang Ngai Prison. There are always several hundred men and women prisoners at the Interrogation Center and well over a thousand at the Quang Ngai Prison. A safe estimate is that 90% of the prisoners in Quang Ngai are being held for political reasons. The severe interrogating and torturing takes place at the Interrogation Center. Most prisoners do not know the charges against them; they haven't had a trial; and they have no knowledge of the length of their jail sentence. CIA personnel in Quang Ngai have been observed frequently visiting the Interrogation Center and it is believed that they provide support and assistance to the Interrogation Center.

From numerous accounts one can conclude that the conditions of confinement, interrogation, and torture in Quang Ngai are repressive and harsh. Whereas much attention and concern has been focused on American Prisoners of War being held in North and South Vietnam, there has been relatively no interest in alleviating the suffering of the many thousands of political prisoners being held by the Saigon government. The United States must assume the major responsibility for these conditions since for many years now the United States has been financing and advising the Vietnamese institutions and personnel running the prison system for the Saigon government.

David and Jane Barton

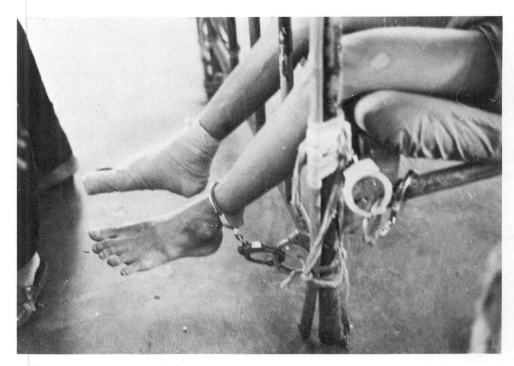

The handcuffs used to shackle this prisoner to his bed in Quang Ngai hospital are made by Smith and Wesson Company of Springfield, Massachusetts.

95

March 21, 1972

To: Commander of National Police, Quang Ngai

Copies to: Senior Province Advisor, National Police Advisor

From: Field Director, Quaker Service Rehabilitation Center, Quang Ngai.

Dear Sir,

This letter is written to inform you of a problem which makes our work at the Quaker Rehabilitation Center difficult. The American Friends Service Committee has a Rehabilitation Center in Quang Ngai in order to provide medical care, physical therapy, and artificial limbs to war-injured civilians regardless of their race, religion, or political views. Currently at our Center we are treating three patients who are handcuffed to their beds. The fact that these three patients are handcuffed to their beds and only released for short periods of time complicates our medical treatment of these patients, prolongs their recovery, and makes their living conditions disagreeable.

The most critical case concerns Tran, a paraplegic, who has been handcuffed to his bed on the Orthopaedic Ward of the Quang Ngai Hospital for 15 months. Because Tran is paralyzed from the waist down he has no control over his urinary and bowel functions. This incontinent problem is obviously complicated by his being handcuffed to his bed. Also as a paraplegic patient Tran has been trained to continually change his body position while lying in bed otherwise he is likely to develop bed sores which are quite susceptible to serious infections. Such bed sores are a common cause of death among paraplegic patients. Being handcuffed to his hospital bed severely inhibits his ability to continually change positions thus increasing the likelihood of bed sores. A paraplegic patient should also exercise several times daily with his braces in our Physical Therapy Department if there is to be any progress in increasing the patient's chances for a longer, healthier life. Currently, he is only released for one or two short periods of time a day during the week to come to our Center for physical therapy. This is insufficient. Because of his paralysis Tran faces a daily struggle to survive and improve his chances for a longer, healthier life. For medical reasons and for reasons of human concern this man should not be handcuffed to his bed. Ever since arriving at the hospital, 15 months ago, he has been handcuffed to his bed not knowing why nor by whom he was being held captive.

This is the same case as with the other two patients who have also been handcuffed to their beds ever since arriving at the Quang Ngai Hospital. Both Le and PCT do not know why nor by whom they are being held. Le has had his left leg amputated above the knee and half his right foot amputated. He has been handcuffed to his bed for 11 months. He is staying at the Quaker Hostel. At the Rehabilitation Center he has been fitted for his artificial leg and he is now gait training before the leg is finished. PCT has been handcuffed to his bed on Ward C of the Quang Ngai Hospital for 13 months. He is currently receiving physical therapy at our Center because of the severe fractures to his leg and the resulting fixed knee. These two patients, Le and PCT, are also not released frequently enough to allow for proper medical, physical therapy, and prosthetic care. Because they are handcuffed to their beds except for the one or two brief periods they are released daily during the week their living conditions are uncomfortable and difficult.

As I think you can realize from these brief descriptions, the practice of handcuffing or chaining patients to their beds for long periods of time without their knowing why nor by whom they are being held causes many serious problems. I would like to respectfully request that this practice be discontinued immediately. I am most willing to be consulted and questioned further as to possible solutions to this problem.

David Paul Barton

<u>Letter from the Quaker Team in Quang Ngai to Philadelphia AFSC, March 22, 1972</u>

I've finally gotten things moving on the patient/prisoner issue. Enclosed is a letter I've delivered to the American advisor to the Quang Ngai branch of the National Police, Kenneth Burns, and also to the American Senior Province Advisor, Colonel McGowen. These two copies were sent to them for their information as I am really trying to deal directly with the Vietnamese authorities who are responsible. As usual in the complicated scene here it took awhile to determine exactly who those responsible parties were. The three patients mentioned are being handcuffed to their beds by the director of the Province Interrogation Center (PIC) but in order for the policy to be changed one must speak to his superior who is the Commander of the National Police. So, letters have been written in Vietnamese /to them/ and a copy sent to the Province Chief.

Michael Jones /American Friends Service Committee representative in Saigon/ and I have already been working a full week on this and we have yet to meet the Commander of the National Police or the Director of the PIC, but we have discussed the problem with their subordinates. Due to the difficulty in meeting them we decided to put something in writing before them to hopefully stimulate a little action and concern on their part. Apparently the Americans are quite concerned especially since Tom Fox of the <u>New York Times</u> was here and after talking with us he questioned Colonel McGowen about the practice of chaining and handcuffing patients to their beds. Nothing like the threat of a little bad press... The National Police Advisor told us that he has already secured 140,000 piasters to improve the prison ward at the Quang Ngai Hospital. He plans to redo it with new screens, doors, johns, locks, etc. so that the patient/prisoners can be unchained and a 24-hour guard stationed there. Not too creative nor innovative but it will be an improvement if it is actually done. We will keep an eye on it.

The pattern seems to be the same on these three prisoners. They were injured in what was perhaps considered an "insecure area," taken to ChuLai, treated, probably labeled "VC" by the Americans and then transported by American chopper from ChuLai to the Quang Ngai Hospital, and then handcuffed upon arrival here. The Americans in ChuLai undoubtedly informed the PIC people here that these were dangerous "VC" and thus the PIC people handcuffed them until they were ready for interrogation. . . .

Also hope to send a photo and letter to Smith & Wesson Co. in Springfield, Mass. so that they can see how their handcuffs are being used in Vietnam.

<u>Letter from the Quaker Team in Quang Ngai to Philadelphia AFSC, June 16, 1972</u>

<u>Patient-Prisoners Freed!</u> Our three handcuffed patients received their release papers the day after Jane and I returned to Quang Ngai. They were elated and so were we but a little reluctant to celebrate not knowing whether or not to believe it. Sure enough that afternoon a Province Interrogation Center guy came by to collect their papers without explanation. Faces dropped. . . But the next morning /he/ returned the papers saying he had taken them only to make sure our dangerous paraplegic, amputee, and fracture patients had been cleared by the PIC interrogators.

Thus far, a week or so later, they are still free and enjoying it by paying occasional evening visits to the Quaker House (a little easier than before when they would have had to bring their beds with them). Perhaps the high Quang Ngai Province authorities did decide that our paraplegic VCI was not an infrastructure but only incontinent, that our amputee-district-terrorist (who wants to take up haircutting) would no longer be able to strike fear into the hearts and minds of his neighbors without his left leg and right foot, and that our fractured femur friend was truly scared when he ran from his rice field to hide behind a rock while ARVNs fired at him and that he had not disposed of his AK-47 by eating it in the meantime.

Report from the Field Co-director, Quaker Service, Quang Ngai, July 30, 1972

WOMEN IN PRISON, QUANG NGAI, VIETNAM

Recently I have been making daily visits to the prison-ward at the Quang Ngai Province Hospital with AFSC medical staff. The ward is a small room where prisoners are brought from the prison or interrogation center. The selection of those prisoners who are allowed to go to the hospital seems to be entirely arbitrary. Some prisoners are gravely ill while others have minor complaints. "Important" or "dangerous" prisoners can never go to the hospital no matter how serious their illness or injury is. There are over two thousand political prisoners currently being held in Quang Ngai, but there are only eight beds in the prison ward. At two bodies a bed, that means only sixteen of these prisoners can be in the hospital at the same time. Even then they don't get treated. No doctor is assigned to or visits the ward. The nurse does change their bandages every few days, but the only medicine the prisoners are ever given is aspirin.

Many people who visit our rehabilitation center empathize with the leg-less children, but I identify most with women of my own age. I've felt particularly troubled at seeing the many young women prisoners at the hospital. These women are chained to their beds and chained together in pairs. Twice a day they are unlocked and released in order to go to the bathroom, but their ankle chains are not undone, so two of them must hobble and awkwardly drag their chains around together. Since I act as the doctor's interpreter, I talk with all the patients as we treat them. Some of the youngest women seem so sweet and naive; they even giggle and laugh a bit. Others are quiet and strong and a few look at me with hostility and hate. One young girl is now on the prison ward at the hospital because she rejected an ARVN officer. This ex-boyfriend had police friends and, in revenge, he told the police that the girl was a "VC." She was taken to the prison where they beat her and repeatedly banged her head against the wall. Later she was given electric shocks under her fingernails. She often blanked out and once when she awoke, she found blood coming from her vagina. Sometime during the torturing, she received nerve damage and she is now a hemiplegic; meaning that half of her body, the left half, is completely paralyzed from the neck down. Also, she has repeated seizures or fits during which she thrashes and convulses, foams at the mouth, and yells the things she must have told the police while she was tortured, such as, "I'm innocent. Ask my villagers, I'm not a VC." I've witnessed several of these seizures. The other prisoners seem to know when they are beginning and tie her legs and arms to the bed with soft bandages. The person who is chained to her tries to move away and someone else keeps the girl from swallowing her tongue. No one says anything. Nor is there a change in anyone's expression in the room. It seems as if the prisoners look on dispassionately, but I'm sure every scene like this increases the other prisoners' bitterness and resolve to struggle. It's well known that the best revolutionaries are made in prison.

Another woman on the ward can't lift her head. She was beaten all over her back and neck. The entire area is exposed raw skin and muscles and in some places the lacerations were so deep, they had to be stitched. Whenever I saw her, she was in a seated position with her head hung down. It wasn't until I saw her lying down that I noticed she was very pregnant; six and a half months she says. I wonder if the baby is alive.

An older woman on the ward called me over to look at herself and a fifteen year old girl. The young girl was totally vacant. She didn't hear or say anything. I kept looking at a necklace she was wearing made of round white stones. It's rare to see Vietnamese women in Quang Ngai with jewelry and it seemed particularly ironic that the police would beat this girl into a coma-like state without stealing or ripping off her necklace. She was a delicate girl in her white blouse and necklace and her hair tied back with a length of hospital gauze. The hot, soapy water the girl had been forced to drink was a toxic which has probably caused brain damage and memory lapses.

The thirty-five year old woman chained to this younger girl had also been beaten and tortured, but she was an old-timer. She even knew Bac Si Mai (Marge Nelson, former team member/doctor) when Marge used to visit the prison. I thought, my god, Marge goes home and testifies before Congress about the torturing she witnessed at the prison, but the same woman who was tortured four years ago is still in prison and still being tortured and no one has done a damned thing about it. I thought, too, about the years this woman has been in jail. Marge has returned to the US, married, finished a master's degree in public health, practiced medicine, had a baby, and talked and traveled in many countries. This woman hasn't gone anywhere or done anything. She says she has been a political prisoner for six years.

Somehow these women persevere, but I wonder if they can do it indefinitely. A Quang Ngai police official told a reporter friend of mine that the police are beginning a special campaign to pick up more women. They suspect that more women than ever are indirectly or directly working to oppose the Thieu government. I imagine that the torture and suffering we've seen at the prison and the prison hospital ward over the last five years is just a glimpse of a new era of struggle for the women of Vietnam.

Jane Leida G. Barton

<u>Letter from the Quaker Team in Quang Ngai, to Philadelphia AFSC, August 3, 1972</u>

John, Phan and I have been visiting the prison ward at the hospital as a temporary alternative to our visiting the prison itself. There is no doubt that many of the prisoners have received cruel and inhumane treatment. Severe beatings or the forced drinking of soapy or white-wash water are the most frequent tortures. Presently we are treating a number of patients such as those I described in the article. Plus there are patients such as a woman who was shot through the chest and now has a lung abscess. Another girl had her leg set so badly, one leg is several inches shorter than the other. She now can't move the leg and thus could really benefit from physical therapy. The bullet which caused her injury is, of course, still in her leg. But worse, the young woman has a severe cardiac problem and without treatment may not have a long time to live. Because returning to prison or another beating might be fatal, we are trying to get her released though our hopes aren't high. Today we saw a new patient - a chained female prisoner who was crazy, reduced to nonsensical, bizarre behavior. The policeman-guard at the ward ridiculed and laughed at her, sarcastically asking us if we could help her. I suggested to him that she might be better if she had her freedom.

. . . . .

I think our visits to the ward have been "successful." The prisoners are interested in us and pleased we come. The most frustrating and sad aspect is that the prisoners come and go so quickly. One day we will see someone (such as a guy with pneumonia or bad case of TB) and arrive the next day with medicine, but the patient will be gone. Several of the women I wrote about have already been returned to the interrogation center. I felt fond of some and anticipated seeing them, but suddenly they disappear--their bed empty or replaced with a new prisoner.

<u>Letter from the Quaker Team in Quang Ngai, to Philadelphia AFSC, August 27, 1972</u>

<u>Prison Program Quang Ngai</u>: A little history. In April we received a letter from the head of the prison saying we were not allowed to visit the prison anymore for "special reasons" which we assumed, and were also informed, was the result of general tightening of security. Then in June when we returned to Quang Ngai we inquired about the reasons for not continuing our work at the prison and wrote an official letter to the Province Chief. In the meantime John Talmadge and I began making visits to the prison ward at the hospital. As I've already written, we treated a lot of mighty sick people, none of whom were being seen by a doctor.

<u>Torturing</u>: While examining prisoners John and I were convinced that we saw what were the results of torturing. (1) John could determine some of this through physical examination. (2) On occasion John was able to get x-rays to confirm certain injuries such as skull fractures, cracked ribs, etc. (3) This was corroborated with direct information from the prisoners who seemed very free to tell us about the treatment of the police, especially since there wasn't a policeman/guard around a lot of the time. Naturally, the team was most disturbed and angry over the entire situation - being kicked out of the prison, the total lack of medical treatment available to the prisoners, but most of all the torturing we felt the prisoners had suffered. We decided as a team to take whatever cautious steps we could in Quang Ngai to try to correct the situation.

<u>August 1</u>: John, David Paul and I made a visit to see McBride, the Deputy Province Senior Advisor. We stated that the purpose of our visit was to inform him that in our work at the hospital we were seeing prisoners who we felt had been inhumanely treated and wished to bring these facts to his attention. We explained that in our work we prefer to work through Vietnamese channels and planned to see the Province Chief, but wanted the Americans to be aware of our dissatisfaction and intentions. In addition, we made sure that McBride understood the delicacy of our situation since we want to return to the prison and continue to work at the hospital. We told him not to speak to anyone on our behalf. McBride didn't have much of a response except to talk about the cruelty of Orientals. He said torturing "comes to them naturally. They're just not my kind of people." McBride assured us he would relay our conversation to Colonel Boman, the PSA.

<u>August 9</u>: The nurse and I were on our way to visit the prison ward when we were met by two policemen--one from the prison, the other from the interrogation center. They told us that the Quakers were not allowed to visit the prison ward at the hospital anymore. The reason was that since we no longer could see prisoners at the prison, the authorities felt we shouldn't be allowed to treat prisoners at the hospital either. One policeman said that the police and prison officials don't have "confidence" in the Quakers. He also mumbled something about not wanting the prisoners to talk to us. I didn't say much to the policemen at the time since I wanted to talk to the team first and felt, too, that the police were only conveying orders from "higher" up.

<u>August 10</u>: David Paul went to the Province Headquarters to try again to make an appointment with the Province Chief. They met in the hall and David said that we wanted to talk to him, Colonel Loi, about the prison situation. In essence, Colonel Loi's response was that he'd already written us a letter saying the Quakers could not continue to work at the prison "forever". Although David was polite and tried to get Colonel Loi to
·give him the reasons for his actions, Loi was gruff and curt with David. Loi also refused to meet us to discuss the matter personally.

9 9

That afternoon, after checking with the police-guards, John, David and I went to the prison ward at the hospital and spoke publicly to all the prisoners telling them that we were told we could no longer visit the prison ward. We said we were sorry we had to interrupt our medical treatments since we knew many of them were badly in need of medicine, but that we would try our hardest to persuade the authorities to let us continue our work. We were cautious and non-accusatory in what we said, but felt we owed an explanation to the prisoners as to why we'd suddenly terminated our daily medical visits.

<u>August 11:</u> <u>Meeting with Boman:</u> John, David and I met with Colonel Boman, the new PSA, to discuss three problems: (1) our desire to resume our medical visits to the prison, (2) our interest in continuing to work at the prison ward at the hospital, (3) the results of torturing we'd felt we'd witnessed. Colonel Boman spent a lot of time running down all the reasons why the Americans are ignorant of what is going on at the detention center and prison and why they can't change the Vietnamese system very much since the Americans are only advisors and must stay on good terms with their counterparts. Among our rebuttals was the comment that we felt that any country which could wage a war of the magnitude America has in Vietnam surely has the power and resources to change a local prison system. When we didn't seem to be getting anywhere with Colonel Boman, David Paul said that we were trying to work through the Americans and Vietnamese in Quang Ngai, but that if that didn't produce any results, we knew that the press would be interested in the problem and that we would also inform members of Congress. Colonel Boman winced a little and asked David if we were trying to scare him. David replied that we weren't. Quakers worked in the open and we did not want to do anything behind his back. We therefore were informing both the Americans and the Vietnamese about our observations about the treatment of prisoners, but that we were very disturbed over the situation so that if the Americans and Vietnamese couldn't do anything, we would act in ways we felt necessary to correct the situation as we saw it.

<u>Letter from the Province Chief:</u> We received the promised letter from Colonel Loi which thanked us for our past work "in this savage time of war which the communists have brought upon us." The letter went on to say, "We admire your concern for serving the people of Vietnam regardless of their color, race, religion, or politics" (a quote from our letter to him), "but those evil people who kill innocent people yesterday and today, who are treated by your organization, do not change their cruel attitude. I can not grant your request to return to work in the prison." The translation sounds a bit awkward, but even Vietnamese who read the letter were surprised at the bluntness of the implication made in the letter that by giving medical help to prisoners we were helping the communists.

<u>Response from Colonel Boman:</u> Late in the afternoon David Paul spoke to Boman again. Boman said (1) the Quaker prison program was definitely terminated (2) we would be allowed to make visits to the prison ward at the hospital (3) there would be an investigation by the Americans and the Vietnamese about our accusations that some prisoners are being tortured (4) that a Vietnamese doctor would begin making visits to the prison (the same way they do at the hospital, we thought). Colonel Boman elaborated on what Colonel Loi had given as reasons for our not continuing our work at the prison which basically focused on Loi's not liking the Quaker philosophy/politics. Boman quoted Loi as saying we spoke against the Saigon government. Colonel Loi also told Boman that he didn't understand why we wanted to visit the prison when our purpose for being in Vietnam was to do "orthopedic work." The only specific incident Loi mentioned to Boman was that once a Quaker worker told a prisoner that the VC had taken control of areas south of town and cut the highway so the hospital truck with medicines for the prisoners couldn't get through. David responded tactfully and fully to these accusations. For the second time, David explained to Boman the purposes of our work in Quang Ngai and the work of AFSC and Quakers in general. Colonel Boman listened and seemed somewhat understanding, though not in agreement, with our ideas. He had also done a little research of his own and mentioned reading a file on Marge /Dr. Nelson/ and some of her testimony. "She really criticised Quang Ngai up one side and down the other, but of course, when the Americans checked into her accusations, they were all found to be untrue."

<u>August 12:</u> John and I visited the prison ward at the hospital to find that at least a third of the patients had been removed, especially the most seriously sick patients. In fact, only one prisoner who was really in need of treatment was left on the ward. The other prisoners all had minor ailments -- "winds in their chests, heat in the stomach, etc." We were especially concerned to discover the two most seriously ill prisoners were no longer there--a woman with a serious heart problem and bullet in her leg and a young hemiplegic woman with a fractured skull. The police said that both these women, along with the other sick prisoners, were taken back for "further interrogation." Ironically, we had just written letters with John's signature, to the province Chief and head of the Interrogation Center asking for these two women to be released for medical treatment and that "further imprisonment will constitute a definite threat to their life and health." It seemed obvious that now that the Quakers were allowed to visit the prison ward again the police had removed all the very sick patients, particularly those whom we might suspect had been tortured. We wondered if in the future the police would "screen" (more than they do already) those prisoners who would be allowed to go to the hospital and prevent many of those who needed medical help from seeing us.

<u>August 14:</u> David Paul and I confronted Colonel Boman once again to say that we'd felt "double-crossed." Once the Quakers were let back onto the prison ward at the hospital, all of the seriously ill prisoners were removed. We gave him copies in English of the two letters we'd written about the two women prisoners who we felt were currently in danger by being back in the detention center due to their medical conditions. Boman did not make any promises to ensure that the police would not prohibit prisoners who need medical help from coming to the prison, but he did say he would check to see what the Vietnamese were doing about our requests of release of the two prisoners.

<u>Presently:</u> Colonel Boman is currently on vacation, so we've not had further word from him nor have we gotten a response to the letters about the women prisoners from the Americans or Vietnamese. Caroline or I have continued to visit the prison ward with the nurse since John's departure, but the prisoners allowed on the ward continue to only be those with minor complaints.

100

Report from the Field Co-director, Quaker Service, Quang Ngai

NOTES ON SOME PRISONERS TREATED IN THE PRISON WARD, QUANG NGAI PROVINCE HOSPITAL DURING AUGUST, 1972

Pham thi Tho: (See following statement) 18 year old woman. Wounded in Mo Duc. Shot in the thigh and the bullet is still lodged in her leg. Her leg was set at the prison. A cast was on the leg for three months but there was a malunion so that one leg is two inches shorter than the other. While examining the patient, John Talmadge, the AFSC medical staff there , discovered that she had a very irregular heart beat, in John's words "a cardiovascular problem of potentially serious consequence." This patient was in the prison-ward with a temperature for six days, also suffered from nausea, stomach ache, and back pains. She went back to the Province Interrogation Center once for three days but returned with fever and nausea. John Talmadge felt that some of these symptoms might be related to a mild heart attack. This prisoner had also lost muscle control of her foot and leg thus finding it difficult to walk. The AFSC physical therapist, Caroline Elliot, did exercises with the patient on the prison-ward. A bracemaker measured her foot and made her special surgical shoes, but they have never been able to deliver them because the prisoner was removed from the ward. A Doctor An signed the hospital release form for this patient/prisoner but to our knowledge this doctor never visited the prison ward and never examined the patient. On the day our surgical nurse went to prepare this patient for an operation to remove the bullet from her leg, we were told we could no longer visit the prison ward at the hospital. Three days later after we lodged a protest, we were allowed back on the prison-ward of the hospital but this particular prisoner had been sent back to the Interrogation Center in spite of John Talmadge's letter fully explaining his evaluation of this patient's medical condition. Copies of this letter were sent to Colonel Boman, the Senior Province Advisor, and Ken Burns, advisor to the National Police and Vietnamese officials. Thus, they are aware of this prisoner's weakened medical condition. The guards at the prison-ward told us that this patient was a "prisoner-of-war" and had to go back to the Interrogation Center for further questioning.

Nguyen thi Lang: (See following statement) John Talmadge first saw this woman prisoner before visiting the prison ward. A physical therapist found out about the prisoner and brought her to the Center since the prisoner was continually having "fits." One of her complaints was of bleeding from her vagina. A vaginal examination was performed. Then the patient was returned to the prison. Later she was seen again on the prison-ward and she was still continuing to have "fits," as many as ten during the day and night. She was unable to move the right side of her body. Examination showed swelling on the top of her head because, she said, the police had banged her head against a wall. An x-ray was taken and confirmed that she had suffered a skull fracture with resulting paralysis to the right side of her body.

Young boy, 17 years old: Arrived at the prison ward from the Interrogation Center during the time we were not allowed to visit the ward. The boy's father came to the Rehabilitation Center to ask us to help because he had heard the Quakers were "kind." We went to the ward and the police guards were so afraid that the young boy was going to die that they let us in the ward. The boy had not gone to the bathroom for four days (urinated) and was in extreme pain. John Talmadge thought it was a block in the urinary tract but he wanted someone else's assistance on the problem, so Dr. Khai came and assisted in administering medication. Later, we were told that the young boy prisoner had been tortured with electricity attached to his penis.

Two young boys in same bed: One with a mine injury to his foot*, one with a lower leg wound. Both were treated with penicillin and given crutches.

Woman six months pregnant, 34 years old: Neck and back injuries attributed to beatings received at Interrogation Center. Also said she was forced to drink soapy (lime) water solution. On the prison ward for three days then returned to the Interrogation Center.

Woman, 32 years old: Bullet wound piercing her chest and lung. X-ray showed abscess on her lung from bullet wound. We treated with penicillin but the patient was returned to the Interrogation Center before recovery.

Old, wrinkled, skinny man: Extremely swollen neck. John Talmadge diagnosed it as a glandular infection/fever. Forced to return to the Interrogation Center because the police did not have enough handcuffs to lock him to a bed on the ward. We were able to give him a shot of Bicillin, a long-acting penicillin, ordered by John Ferger. We requested that this old man be returned to the hospital for treatment. We never saw him again.

Another old man with a strange paralysis: Unable to raise or move his arms; his legs were also partially paralyzed. Prisoner kept trying to move. Other prisoners on the ward fed and cared for him. Doctor and Physical Therapist puzzled by this paralysis and its cause. In about three days this man was able to stand and he gradually improved.

Man with TB: Deep cough, spitting up blood -- tuberculosis. Suggested that this man go to the public health TB clinic for tests and treatment. He remained on prison ward for six days with the above patients before being taken for tests; then he was returned to the prison.

---

* See letter of August 3, 1972 for more thoughts about this woman and Doctor Nelson.

Young man, age 23:   High fever and sweating. Doctor listened to him breathe and thought this prisoner had either TB or pneumonia. The doctor saw the patient at 5:00 PM but the next morning when the doctor returned to see the patient and give some medication the prisoner had been returned to the Interrogation Center. We requested that the prisoner return for treatment to the hospital but there was no response and the prisoner was never seen again.

Young girl with white-stone necklace: She had "petit mal" seizures and stared into space. She exhibited symptoms of loss of memory. She said she had been forced to drink a white-wash, soapy solution many times while being interrogated.

Young boy,* age 19:   He had been shot thru the palm of his hand which had become very infected and swollen. The prison guard brought this prisoner to the Rehabilitation Center three times for cleansing and treatment of the wound. Bicillin was injected and the infection cleared up thus saving his hand which otherwise would have had to be amputated because of the worsening infection.

Young girl with grey blouse: This prisoner said she had been forced to drink water mixed with a lime/white-wash solution after which the guards jumped on her bloated stomach. She said she had also been beaten with a heavy club. She complained of pain in her chest and stomach. On three occasions this prisoner was observed having fits.

Two young girls: General complaints of aches and chest pains. They had bruises. Both had several fits.

Strong, large woman, age 45:   Also complained of chest pains. Among other tortures she specifically mentioned electricity. This woman had the most dramatic "fits" or "seizures" of all the prisoners. She would thrash violently, yelling, and crying. Her entire body would rise in the air, her back arched, she would then come crashing down on her bed, sometimes causing the bed to move several feet with each violent heave. This woman's seizures would last approximately fifteen minutes.

Another older woman: This woman was chained to the above mentioned woman. This woman said she had been beaten with a club on her chest, neck, and face. Upon examination the doctor observed that her face was severely swollen, her chest and neck were bruised, and her chest x-ray showed cracked ribs. She also related that she had been forced to drink water with lime. This prisoner was unable to walk and had to be helped by other prisoners in order to go to the bathroom. This prisoner also related that she had known Doctor Marge Nelson when Doctor Nelson visited the Quang Ngai prison some four years ago.

Man who never said anything: This prisoner's expressionless, apathetic behavior was explained by other prisoners who said that he had been tortured and beaten so long and so many times that now he didn't know anything and was always in this semi-conscious state.

Crazy Woman: A fairly young woman with close cropped hair. Totally nonsensical behavior, unaware of her surroundings. She moaned, moved her body rhythmically, chanted, smiled, and talked to no one. Other prisoners said she hadn't been crazy before she was put in prison. Upon examination she seemed to have nothing medically wrong with her.

Jane Leida G. Barton

Two prisoners at the Quang Ngai hospital prison ward. On the right is the "man who never said anything."

*The prisoners with the asterisks by their descriptions were the only two prisoners remaining on the prison-ward of the hospital when the AFSC Team in Quang Ngai was allowed back on the prison-ward.

August 8, 1972

PATIENT'S FULL NAME: _____Pham thi Tho_____

TO WHOM IT MAY CONCERN:

On August 1, 1972, I examined the patient and determined that she has a cardiovascular problem of potentially serious consequence. There is a definite and unmistakable irregularity in the rhythm of her heart, and further diagnostic studies are necessary in order to provide her with appropriate medical care.

In addition to her grave cardiac status, this patient has a fractured femur secondary to a bullet wound; the bullet has not been removed, and she has received only marginally adequate orthopaedic attention. At present she is unable to walk and would benefit significantly from physical therapy at the Quaker Center. Our surgical team can also evaluate the status of her bullet wound and perhaps extract the bullet itself.

I strongly recommend that this patient's case be reviewed and that she be released from detention in order that she may receive proper medical treatment. Her further imprisonment will constitute a definite threat to her life and health.

Sincerely,

John Mills Talmadge, Jr.

August 8, 1972

PATIENT'S FULL NAME: _____Nguyen thi Lang_____

TO WHOM IT MAY CONCERN:

The woman whose name appears above has been under my care for the past month. She suffers from a persistent right-sided hemiplegia which is secondary to acute cerebral trauma incurred during recent detention for interrogation. In addition she manifests symptoms of more complex neurologic disorder; it is not possible to diagnose and evaluate her case properly in her present confined state, nor is it possible to provide her with any rehabilitative therapy which might restore the use of her right arm and leg.

I strongly recommend that this patient's case be reviewed and that she be released from detention in order that she may receive proper medical treatment. Her further imprisonment will constitute a definite threat to any chance of returning her to a normal, healthy life.

Sincerely,

John Mills Talmadge, Jr.

LETTER TO VICE PRESIDENT AGNEW
(Written at the time of his visit to Vietnam in August, 1970)

Committee Of Women's Movement For The Right To Life

Chairman of the Presidential Committee
2 Cao-Ba-Quat, Saigon

To Mr. Spiro Agnew
Vice President
of the United States of America
c/o the U.S. Embassy
Saigon

Dear Mr. Vice President,

We know that your visit to Vietnam is connected with the making of important decisions. We also know that you are a father, the head of a family. As a father, you have deep love towards your children and you have experienced moments of anxiety when your children are in danger. As a leader of your country, you have many concerns on the South Vietnamese Government action. It is with this knowledge that we are taking the liberty to write to you this letter.

We are the Mothers of the political prisoners detained in the various prisons of South Vietnam. None of our children are convicted of crime or robbery. All of them are being imprisoned because they have dared to speak of Peace and Independence, a most profound desire of all the Vetinamese people after years of war. Our children were arrested and barbarously tortured. They have been denied food and drink, even medicine when they are sick. The limited amount of medicine provided to the prisoners by the American aid have been continuously smuggled or stolen by the prison authorities. We only learn about the terrible living conditions of our children through statements by recently released prisoners and reports made by the U.S. Representatives ANDERSON and HAWKINS after their investigation of Con Son Tiger Cages and the living conditions of the prisoners.

Hcwever, up to the present time, we still have not been allowed to visit or keep in touch with our children despite renewed requests. We have no means to send food to them at all. Only one exception has been given to those mothers who were allowed to visit their children once on August 25th, 1970 at the Chi Hoa prison. We have witnessed our children's health situation. After continuous beatings, their bodies were swollen; when they were allowed to see us, they could not even walk and had to be helped by two guards. Such is the actual result of our government system of repression.

Most of our children were tried by the Military Field Court, a Court which was held unconstitutional by the Supreme Court. Yet, our children have not been released. Some of them have never been tried at all.

As a father, as a leader, you are coming to Vietnam to understand out people's aspirations for Peace and Justice. We, the Vietnamese Mothers, want to speak out the terrible sufferings of thousands of mothers who have their children being tortured and ill-treated in jail. We wish to directly inform you about the crimes committed under the prison system of South Vietnam. <u>We hope to have privilege of meeting you while you are here</u>.

You would have to agree that the U.S. Government somehow has to be held jointly responsible for the prison system in South Vietnam, since:

- The police forces which arrest and repress our children are being paid by the Americans.

- The equipment used by the Police to repress, torture and jail our children are part of the U.S. aid. The tear gas, the rockets used to repress them are "made in U.S.A.". We actually witnessed the terrible repression being carried out right in front of the U.S. Embassy when we and our foreign friends demonstrated against the prison system on July 11th, 1970.

- The Phoenix Operation, the result of which a great number of "suspected" Vietnamese people have been arbitrarily arrested and imprisoned directly by American authorities in Saigon.

- In the military operations, U.S. and Allied Forces have arrested and tortured many innocent Vietnamese farmers at the Intelligence Agencies or turned them to the South Vietnamese government for further detention without any "due process of law."

- Our children witness the presence of American Advisors at the prisons. They know that more aid is being given to build more and bigger prisons.

Before such evidence it would be hard to deny and just say that the U.S. is not responsible for the prison system of South Vietnam. The role of the American advisors should be to improve the prisoners conditions, not watch the tortures done to our children who suffer from hunger, thirst, disease, and survive in agony in jail.

We wish to meet you and let you know more specifically about our concern. May we ask you to convey to President NIXON, the American Government and the U.S. Congress our requests that urgent improvement on the prison system can be done. Our requests are primarily the following:

1. No citizen shall be arrested without lawful ground
2. All prisoners should be provided with proper food and drink, and should be given appropriate care when they are sick.
3. The prisoners relatives should be allowed to correspond, visit and send extra supply to the prisoners.
4. The prisoners should be allowed to write to their families
5. Relatives of prisoners should be immediately reported when the prisoners are arrested
6. Corruption practice in prison should be immediately abolished so that our children's food rations are not taken away.
7. The present policy of using non-political prisoners (criminals, thieves..) to watch political prisoners should be immediately abolished.
8. Our children should be allowed to do some reading in jail for their own culture
9. The prisoners whose jail terms have expired must be immediately released.
10. Those prisoners who have not been tried should be released or put on further trial by a constitutional, civil court.
11. Those prisoners who were tried by the Military Field Courts should be released or retried by a civil court if they are supposed to be guilty.
12. The old, sick and under-age prisoners should be released.
13. There should be a change in the jail staff system
14. Tiger cages, Cattle cages, mysterious caves, separate cells, discipline cells and rooms used for inhumane tortures should be abolished, not only at Con Son but also in all the prisons throughout South Vietnam.
15. The "Coolies of the Battle-fields" system used for military prisoners and "released" political prisoners should be abolished.
16. When a prisoner dies, his body should be returned to his family for proper burial.

We also ask you to urge the American authorities to immediately end their acts of cruelty toward political prisoners and instruct them about our above mentioned requests.

In short, we want our children to have enough food, drink, and medicine; their physical as well as moral life to be decently dealt with. They are not criminals but young courageous people who dared to stand up and voice for Peace. PEACE IS THE DEEPEST ASPIRATION OF ALL THE VIETNAMESE PEOPLE. Therefore, our children who are struggling for the cause of Peace and have been arrested and barbarously tortured should be considered as "PEACE HEROES."

Hoping that thanks to your responsible and official intervention, our children will soon be removed from the present inhuman prison system of South Vietnam, may we convey to your family our best wishes of luck and happiness.

Respectfully yours,

Representatives of the Mothers whose children are being detained in the various prisons throughout South Vietnam, in the Tiger Cages, in the Disciplinary Cells...without trial or tried by unconstitutional Courts, or have served their jail-term or have been arrested during military operations (U.S., V.N., Allied).

MOTHERS	SON OR DAUGHTER	CITIES
Dang thi Muoi	Vo Van Sau	Long An
Nguyen thi Thanh	Le thi Chi	Nha Be
Nguyen thi Nang	Tran thi Son	Binh Duong
Bui thi Diep	Le thi Kim Nang	Binh Dinh
Nguyen thi Van	Lua Ngoc Chan	Saigon
Vo thi Sam	Luu van An	Bien Hoa
Dang Thi Nguot	Nguyen van Coi	Ban Me Thuct
Nguyen thi Trinh	Nguyen Dinh Tau	Phu Xuan
Nguyen thi Anh	Le Tan Viet Nam	Gia Dinh
Nguyen thi Yen	Dang Thien (sister)	Da Nang
Nguyen thi Nhu	Nguyen Truong Con (brother)	Hue
Nguyen thi Ban	Nguyen van Tam	Tay Ninh
Vo thi Khai	Vo thi Gioi	Chi Hoa
Phan thi Cam	Tran van Thien	Dien Ban
Khong thi Kim	Tu Thu	Vinh Long
Vo thi Tu	Le Anh Ton	Cho Lon
Nguyen thi Binh	Thieu thi Tao	Saigon
	Thieu thi Tam	Saigon
Dang thi Banh	Hoang thi Kim Ngan	Saigon
	Dang cong Tam (son-in-law)	Saigon
Vo thi Ti	Cao thi Hot	Saigon
	Phan Dinh Hoat (son-in-law)	Saigon
Dang thi Hoang	Nguyen thi Danh	Cho Lon
Le thi Ve	Pham Lang (husband)	Saigon

For the COMMITTEE OF WOMEN'S MOVEMENT
FOR THE RIGHT TO LIFE
CHAIRMAN OF THE PRESIDENTIAL COMMITTEE

Mrs. NGO BA THANH

(Editorial Note: Neither Mrs. Thanh nor any of the 21 women were allowed to meet with Vice President Agnew. Mrs. Thanh, who has a degree in international law from Columbia and speaks fluent English, requested to talk with Vice President Agnew on the phone. This request was also denied.)

LETTER TO PRESIDENT NIXON

April 12, 1971
Saigon

To: President Richard Milhous Nixon
    The White House
    Washington, D.C.
    U.S.A.
    (through the intermediary of the Committee
     for the Reform of the Prison Regime in
     South Vietnam.)

Mr. President,

Knowing that you share the responsibility for the severity of the prison regime in South Vietnam, knowing that you are paying special attention to all people deprived of liberty since many times in the past you have asked for the liberty of the Americans imprisoned by the North Vietnamese, we, the relatives of the Vietnamese arrested and incarcerated in detention camps and in prisons throughout South Vietnam, are sending this letter in order to present to you the painful realities of the prison regime in South Vietnam and ask you to take urgent action:

1) Throughout South Vietnam, US intelligence agencies have been participating in the incarceration of the Vietnamese and are using systematically all the refined and scientific methods of torture in order to extract forcefully declarations of guilt and thus encroach upon human dignity and oppose the Declaration of Human Rights. As a result, many Vietnamese have become sick or disabled, died or secretly killed, the facts being hidden to the public through a curtain of secrecy.

2) The interrogation centers belonging to the security system of the Republic of Vietnam government are now incarcerating the suspects, arrested without any proof of guilt or with the only proof of being guilty for "loving their country and fighting for peace in Vietnam." These people are tortured in an utterly savage manner in order to obtain their declaration and constituting their file or false proofs of guilt are devised against them and sent to the tribunal.

3) The prisoners are ill-treated, repressed and brutally beaten throughout South Vietnam. The South Vietnamese administration is using the means provided by the US aid such as tear gas rockets, acid, etc. in order to repress the prisoners. Many prisoners have died or became sick or disabled because of these repressions.

4) Prisons are too narrow, dirty and too crowded, with not enough air for breath. In many prisons, typical of which are the tiger cages in Con Son, the prisoners are shackled day and night so that some of them have become paralysed. Presently your government is helping with money and other means in the construction of new tiger cages in Con Son. This has disturbed and angered us as well as the people of Vietnam.

5) The communication between us and our relatives in prison has been limited to the minimum or forbidden completely. Many of us have been denied permission to visit our relatives or to receive letters from them. Our demands are ignored by the government, sometimes we have been repressed (for example the repression occurred on March 19, 1970 in front of the Lower House.)

6) The food in prisons is too poor, composed mainly of rotten rice and bitter dry fish. Medicines are lacking. As a consequence, the majority of prisoners have lung disease, mental disease, paralysis or beri beri.

7) Many people have been arrested and incarcerated for months or for years without trial or sentence or continued to be imprisoned under the regime of detention without any valid reason or they may be imprisoned or deported although they are under probation.

8) There are people who are tortured or repressed to death and people who die of sickness in prison without their family being notified.

We have been presenting to you the real happenings in the prisons throughout South Vietnam. From this presentation, you may refer to the prison regime in your country as well as in the other civilised countries in the world. You will see what your aid in human and material resources have contributed to the people of Vietnam.

Presently most prisons in South Vietnam have advisors from your country and have received physical aid from U.S.A. If the material aids serve as a useful purpose, we will never forget your kindness and humanitarianism in helping us against poverty and backwardness. On the contrary, the prisons in South Vietnam being considered as inhuman, we wonder whether your effort and the effort of your administration provoke in us gratefulness or resentment?

Thus, we, the suffering Vietnamese, appeal to your sense of fairness and your sense of responsibility and request you to meet the following demands:

1) Order the employees of your government to end their participation with the government of the Republic of Vietnam in maintaining a prison regime contrary to the conscience and humanitarianism of men and women in the world.

2) Intervene with the government of the Republic of Vietnam in satisfying our following demands:

   a) Free all the people detained illegally or without evidence for the purpose of terrorizing and repressing the Vietnamese peace-loving patriots. Free the people who are detained without sentence or with expired sentences, the people who are on provation, the people who are old, sick and the small children.

   b) Follow a policy of treating the prisoners with humanitarianism, change completely the present erroneous approach as regarding food, living facilities, clothes, medicines, spiritual activities, the methods of repressing, terrorizing and brutalizing the prisoners.

Anxious to safeguard the rights to life of our relatives, with the convictions that the right and the humanitarian will be accomplished, we wish you to accept our sincere thanks.

Respectfully yours

The representatives of relatives of prisoners in South Vietnam

Nguyen Thi Binh*
Huynh Thi Hoa

Total signatures: 117

* Nguyen Thi Binh is not related to the Prime Minister of the NLF.

BUILD SCHOOLS INSTEAD OF PRISONS

The Chairman of   May 8, 1971
United States Senate
Foreign Relations Committee

We are convinced that the principle of legality is the foundation of true democracy - yet we see that in South Vietnam the law is trampled under foot, prison and detention camps are hellish places aiming at punishing the guilty and the guiltless alike and where people are humiliated, exploited, tortured and shackled in narrow, dark and filthy cells. People are apprehended anywhere, anytime by any security agency, without being permitted to notify their relatives and without knowing their offense, in defiance of all legal procedures. Prisons detain suspects, untried and acquitted defendants, offenders who have received suspended sentences or served their terms, juvenile offenders, old and disabled persons, pregnant women and nursing mothers.

We are convinced that the prison regime is one of the heart-rending aspects of the brutalizing war in South Vietnam. The vestiges of the present dehumanizing prison system will be abolished, the suffering of the Vietnamese people will end only when peace is restored to our land.

We are also convinced that the Vietnamese people have the right to self-determination and that the American people and their representatives in both houses of Congress will whole-heartedly support us in the struggle for this right if they know how the American intervention has brought poverty, loss of human dignity, destruction of traditional culture, suffering and death to our people - yet the American government is not only waging a war in Vietnam, it is also building prisons and detention camps, manning and supporting the barbarous interrogation centers, providing funds and advisors to centers of detention and torture. In 1970, the American government provided funds for security equivalent to three times the funds provided for education, that is U.S. dollars 20.9 million as compared to U.S. dollars 6.1 million. We do not invent these figures, they are taken from the report of your Ambassador in Vietnam. At this very moment, a U. S. firm is constructing isolation cells in Con Son island at the cost of more than U.S. dollars 300,000 to U. S. tax payers.

Motivated by these convictions, we earnestly appeal to you, distinguished chairman of the Senate Foreign Relations Committee and all members of the Committee, to tell the truth to the American people. The truth is revealed in what we mentioned above, the truth is revealed in the eyes of the sixty years old Ba Sau who became blind because of lime thrown into the tiger cages and which we can see in photographs taken by two U.S. Representatives and published by LIFE magazine; the truth is revealed by the death at the Thu Duc detention camps on August 5, 1970 of the still breast-fed little Man who was taken into prison with his mother and who died because no medical care was given to him; the truth is revealed by the girl peasant Tran thi Nga who was tortured to death and whose burial ceremony attended by thousands of people including the members of our Committee that was broken up by the police force. The truth is revealed in a letter dated April 12, 1971, by relatives of prisoners in South Vietnam addressed to U.S. President Richard M. Nixon in which they said that their relatives were arrested without any proof of guilt or with the only truth of being guilty for "loving their country or fighting for peace in Vietnam." The truth is revealed in many cases for which we obtain concrete evidence, however the total truth can never be known but only guessed with thousands upon thousands of inhuman acts perpetrated against prisoners behind a curtain of secrecy.

We appeal to you to ask your government to stop at once the construction of isolation cells in Con Son island, to deny funds and advisors to the Vietnamese government for running prisons, detention camps and interrogation centers. Your government should help us to build schools instead of prisons, to improve our prison regime instead of brutalizing and terrorizing prisoners. We know that the American people are anxious to see U.S. prisoners in North Vietnam be treated humanely, we also earnestly wish so. We believe that the best way to achieve this desire is for the American people to urge their government to provide a decent treatment of prisoners of war and political prisoners in South Vietnam. The U.S. government as well as the VN government should regard political prisoners as those in opposition to the government in power and not as guilty persons, and thus treat them with respect for their dignity and personality.

Finally we appeal to you to unite with us in our campaign for restoring peace and justice in Vietnam.

Respectfully yours,

Professor Nguyen Van Trung
Chrmn., Committee for the Improvement
of the Prison Regime in South Vietnam